FABULOUS FACADES

create breathtaking quilts with fused fabric

GLORIA LOUGHMAN

C&T PUBLISHING

Publisher: Amy Marson

Creative Director: Gailen Runge

Editor: Lynn Koolish

Technical Editor: Debbie Rodgers

Cover/Book Designer: April Mostek

Production Coordinator: Tim Manibusan

Production Editor: Alice Mace Nakanishi

Illustrator: Mary E. Flynn

Photo Assistants: Carly Jean Marin and Mai Yong Vang

Photography by Tony Loughman, unless otherwise noted

Published by C&T Publishing, Inc., P.O. Box 1456, Lafayette, CA 94549

Library of Congress Cataloging-in-Publication Data

Names: Loughman, Gloria, 1949- author.

Title: Fabulous facades : create breathtaking quilts with fused fabric / Gloria Loughman.

Description: Lafayette, California : C&T Publishing, Inc., 2017. | Includes bibliographical references.

Identifiers: LCCN 2016059347 | ISBN 9781617453441 (soft cover)

Subjects: LCSH: Patchwork--Patterns. | Quilting--Patterns. | Fusible materials in sewing.

Classification: LCC TT835 .L685 2017 | DDC 746.46--dc23

LC record available at https://lccn.loc.gov/2016059347

Printed in China

10 9 8 7 6 5 4 3 2 1

Dedication

I dedicate this book to my mother, Florence Jeffery, who sadly passed away while this book was being written. A keen sewer, she resisted quilting for many years as in her own words, she "didn't want to become addicted to patchwork" like I was. She went on to make hundreds of quilts, most of which were given to great-grandchildren, Ronald McDonald House, and many nursing homes.

I also dedicate this book to our two youngest grandchildren, Matilda and Dashiell. With our grandchildren now totaling nine, they are all a never-ending source of joy and add a wonderful dimension and richness to our busy lives.

Acknowledgments

A big thank-you to C&T for undertaking the publication of this book. My friend and editor for a fourth time, Lynn Koolish, has continued to be a wonderful source of encouragement and wisdom. I really appreciated her skills, support, and patience, as we worked together over the last twelve months. I would also like to acknowledge the work of my technical editor, Debbie Rodgers, whose positive comments and commitment to detail have been invaluable.

To the quiltmakers whose work is showcased in the book, a special thank-you. Your stunning quilts have added further depth and are a unique and exciting feature.

Thank you also to our daughters, Amanda, Sarah, and Rebecca. Your continued love, practical support, and encouragement, especially over this last year, has allowed and indeed inspired me to follow my artistic endeavors.

And finally, thank you to my husband, Tony—incredible photographer, enthusiastic traveling companion, helpful critic and sounding board, computer guru and best friend. What a great journey we have had together! Your advice, positive thinking, incredible support and love has meant so much to me as we have worked on this book together.

CONTENTS

INTRODUCTION

When looking at the work of artists, it is interesting to see the progression of themes and techniques as they work along a path that becomes a lifetime journey. There are the easy, downhill sections, where ideas flow and the work is produced quickly and then there is the uphill struggle where nothing seems to work and the progress is really slow. External factors impact on design choices. A holiday to a location full of inspiring scenery, attending an exhibition of another artist's work or a captured moment in time, can be the kick-start that sends us off in another direction.

My quilts up to this point have been based on the landscape. Organic shapes, vivid color schemes, and experimenting with abstraction and pattern, have all been features of my work. A number of factors

Rose Seidler House by Gloria Loughman, 42″ × 54″ (107 cm × 137 cm)

then occurred that had a dramatic impact on the direction of my work. Our eldest daughter returned to university to study architecture. My husband, a keen photographer, printed some superb photos of buildings, and I found within me an appreciation of these structures, which I was very keen to capture in fabric.

I have always loved artwork produced using wood-block or linoleum block (also known as *lino* or *linocut*) printing techniques. The construction process outlined in this book leads to a design that is reminiscent of a linoleum print. Each main shape is outlined with fine dark lines, which add strength and a more graphic feel to the work.

As part of the construction process, the original building is broken down into key shapes. Each of these shapes or segments—be it a wall, doorway, or decorative element—is then constructed on its own base of black or very dark fabric.

As part of the construction process, the original building is broken down into key shapes. Each of these shapes or segments—be it a wall, doorway, or decorative element—is then constructed on its own base of black or very dark fabric. This way the different sections are easily managed and can be stitched easily and with precision. When all the pieces of the facade and background have been completed, they are appliquéd together on the quilt sandwich using fusible web. As each piece of the facade is added in order, you have the feeling you are constructing your own building. Many times, I have watched the delight on students' faces as the final shapes are added and their design comes together.

It must be incredible to be an architect and see your design come to fruition. Builders must also gain an immense sense of satisfaction when their buildings are completed. This technique will allow you to create your own facade and I am sure you will feel a similar sense of achievement.

While the word *facade* is generally used to refer to the front of a building, you can use this construction technique to create other subjects, such as old cars, ships, or any other structure or vehicle, that have a surface area. I have included an example using the outlining technique to construct a container ship (see Cargo Ship Design, page 79) and you can make your own old hippie *Campervan* (page 115).

Always fascinated by pattern, I also took inspiration from tall buildings to make a series of quilts based on skyscrapers. Focusing on the repeated block used for their construction, I filled in the shapes with colored fabrics and stitching. Based on a single block, these quilts have a traditional feel about them but with their dark outlines, they are also quite modern.

As you browse through this book, I am sure your first reaction will be one of pleasure and anticipation as you view many of the wonderful inspirational photographs taken by my husband, Tony. I have been very fortunate to have been invited to teach in some incredibly beautiful places and others, not quite so picturesque, but full of character. I am excited by the patterns and shapes in the big cities and some of their amazing, gravity-defying architecture. I am also unreservedly captivated by old, patched-up houses with clashing color schemes that I am sure have an amazing story to tell. Sometimes, I just can't wait to get home and try to reproduce these treasures in fabric.

After enjoying the visual feast of the inspiring images included, your next thought might be that it is too complicated. A lot of diagrams and instructions. With this thought in mind, I decided to include this image of a quilt made by my granddaughter, Charli, when she was 11. Made as a gift for her parents, it is based on the bathing boxes at a beach near her home. Each box is constructed separately on its own dark base and then stitched to the background. She was able to manage the stitching on the small pieces quite easily and then fused everything down, including the binding! I have also included her most recent quilt, made when she was 12, *Eureka Graffiti* (page 41).

Brighton Bathing Boxes by Charli Bakker, 26″ × 18½″ (66 cm × 47 cm)

I encourage you to have a go at it. It may be your childhood home, the old caravan your parents owned, the incredible skyscraper in your city, or the tumbled-down cottage across the way. All of these are wonderful subjects and deserve to be created in fabric.

I hope you enjoy this book and take up the challenge of making your own facades quilt. My husband and I loved the journey of wandering cities, photographing amazing buildings. Then came my time in the studio, attempting to capture the essence of a facade and its surrounds—still playing with color and pattern, still experimenting with abstraction in backgrounds, always learning and looking forward to starting the next quilt.

HOW TO USE THIS BOOK

Getting started is easy—use one of the projects in the book or download the patterns for many of the construction technique examples and follow along (look for Bonus Download!). All patterns in this book and the Bonus Download! patterns are available at:

tinyurl.com/11200-patterns-download

I suggest you definitely read and/or work through the first example (*Seaside Cottage*, page 51) for a detailed view of the construction techniques. The remaining examples provide additional techniques for various features.

In any case, be sure to read about Design (next page) and Color (page 22)—the valuable information contained is relevant and helpful for any style of quiltmaking.

DESIGN

Buildings feature a huge variety of architectural styles with each country having different types of houses. Some buildings are rural, others are more urban. Buildings have been constructed for many different reasons—airports, farm buildings, churches, boat yards, shops, sporting pavilions, and houses are just a few of the different types of buildings constructed around the world.

Wonky house in Cap-aux-Meules in Quebec's Magdalen Islands

Old railway station in Aveiro, Portugal

Public toilets in Geraldton, Western Australia

Mosque in Abu Dhabi

Ponte Vecchio (old bridge) in Florence, Italy

Interesting residence in Newport, Rhode Island

Changing Rooms at the Geelong Outdoor Sea Baths by Gloria Loughman, 31″ × 45″ (79 cm × 114 cm)

OLD BUILDINGS

Many buildings have a story to tell, especially older buildings that have withstood the test of time. Over the years they have been exposed to the elements—hot sun, torrential rain, powerful earthquakes, freezing temperatures, and snow. They have been ravaged by fire, vandalized with graffiti, and subjected to human neglect. Some buildings have been reduced to a pile of rubble, while others are still bravely standing. Sometimes over the years, inhabitants have tried to patch up the damage, mending broken windows with boards, tin, or even bricks. Holes in walls have been filled in and a patchwork of painted colors have been applied to the walls and windows to liven up the neighborhood.

Fascinating old building in Aveiro, Portugal

Boarded up old doorway in Pisa

Rustic old window

NEW BUILDINGS

New buildings tend to have strong sharp edges and bright shiny surfaces. Unstained by pollution, their brickwork is still clean. They tend to have larger areas of glass and their building materials are more advanced. Using a new building as your source could result in a boring and uninteresting design, but a way to get around this is to focus on a particular aspect such as the windows or the pattern of the girders. Reproducing clouds or buildings reflected in the windows is a wonderful image to portray in fabric. The interplay of the symmetry and hard lines of the windows with the organic nature of the clouds or the distortion of the reflected buildings can be the basis for a strong design.

So with so many exciting possibilities out there, where do you start?

Attractive modern buildings in New York

Colorful skyscraper in Melbourne

Distorted reflections of buildings in San Francisco

CHOOSING YOUR FACADE

When you start to look at buildings with fresh eyes, look past the neglect and disrepair, search out facades full of character to feature in your work. There are also many incredible modern buildings that can inspire you. *Groundbreaking*, *unique*, and *dazzling* are only a few adjectives that can be used to describe some of the stunning buildings constructed in recent times.

When making a quilt based on the facade of a building, it is a good idea to start with a simple design. Choose a building that has simple lines but still has character, with something interesting you can use as a focal point, such as a window, doorway, or lamppost. Alternatively, if the building you just love and want to make is quite complicated, select a slice of the building, making sure you include an area of interest.

Slice of interesting building in Quebec

ELEMENTS OF DESIGN

When assessing your images, keep in mind the various elements of design. These are really the building blocks that you use and combine to build your image.

Line

A line is a path that connects two points. It can be an actual line that has length and width, or an implied line, when two shapes overlap and an edge is created. Combining lines with shapes (page 12) is the basis of design. When you do it well, you can create powerful and intriguing designs.

Lines can be used to separate shapes or to join pieces and direct visual movement. The technique outlined in this book uses

Grid of lines in leaded glass window

Pattern of lines showcased in wrought iron gates, Florence

Lines in an old doorway

line as a major element. Just as in the style of a wood-block print, in which each shape is outlined with a dark line, the shapes that you use to construct your buildings will also be outlined. This dark line around the edge gives the image a graphic feel, providing drama and strength to your design. It accentuates the crucial shapes and elements.

Lines are often used in the detail on buildings—lines around brickwork and decorative elements, such as wrought iron, timber fretwork, and leadlight windows

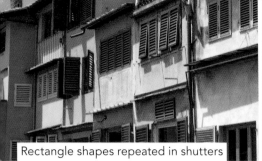
Rectangle shapes repeated in shutters

Box shapes repeated in community housing complex at Habitat 67 in Montreal

Organic shapes of sails on Sydney Opera House

Shape

A shape is an enclosed space with boundaries defined by elements such as lines, colors, values, or textures. Shapes can be geometric or organic. Geometric shapes have clear edges and include triangles, cones, rectangles, and squares. Most geometric shapes have been created by humans, often using tools to achieve accuracy. Architectural shapes are usually rigid with hard edges and based on geometric shapes. Although in recent times, incredible buildings have been constructed that have an organic feel.

Organic shapes are less defined than geometric ones, often with a natural, flowing and curving appearance. They are typically irregular and asymmetrical. They are associated with things from the natural world such as plants and animals.

The area surrounding objects has shape too—this negative space can be very striking and sometimes creates more impact than the original shape.

Triangles and squares dominate the facade of this beautiful old building in Quebec.

Photo by C&T Publishing

Study in Compound Curves by Joan Stogis, 35˝ × 20˝ (89 cm × 51 cm)

Texture

Textures add interest and intrigue to your work. Our sense of touch is stimulated by the element of visual texture, used by artists to create an illusion, such as a rough crumbled wall, lichen on bricks, rust on metal, or shiny glass. Sensory responses demand attention as they invite the viewer in for a closer look.

Texture is a wonderful element of design but must be used wisely. Be careful that the textured areas don't dominate but provide extra interest and focus.

Wonderful texture of lichen and wood

Detail of rust on ship

Fabulous texture of terracotta roof tiles

USING THE ELEMENTS OF DESIGN

Using the elements of design as your building blocks, there are a number of important design principles to keep in mind as you plan your composition.

contribute to the image?" If it is a distraction, leave it out. You might also decide to simplify the background to draw attention to the building. Learning to edit your work will result in a much stronger composition and is a liberating experience.

Editing

It is easy to be overwhelmed by an image, so you need to edit out unnecessary details. If your scene features a streetscape of buildings, select two or three elements to tell the story. Evaluate all the parts of the scene to see what contributes to the overall design. Choose the elements you love and eliminate others that are not essential or don't add to the design. Ask yourself questions such as, "Does the power pole

Eliminating power lines would improve this image of old and new in Melbourne.

Exaggeration

Just as you have artistic license to eliminate, you also can make a statement through exaggeration—overstating reality can certainly attract attention. Manipulating size differences, adding saturated color, or even outrageous distortion—anything that exaggerates or magnifies certain elements can add something special to your design.

Repetition

Repetition is a powerful design tool. Any design element can be repeated for strong visual effect. Repetition also provides movement (page 16).

Repetition of Shape

Building facades often feature repeating shapes. Once you start observing, you quickly realize that the urban landscape is full of patterns. Windows, roofs, lampposts, and even the outline of buildings themselves, provide the artist with wonderful repetitions of shapes. Any time you use a recurring pattern or line it draws attention. Repetition can be the attention grabber itself or it can be used to direct the viewer's eye toward a specific area. Just be careful that repetition doesn't lead the eye away from the main center of interest or, indeed, overwhelm it.

Repeated archways draw attention in Mosque, Abu Dhabi.

Repetition of Color

Repeating colors is one way to bring unity to your work. The effect of color repetition can be accomplished in a number of ways: using the same color in multiple places, using analogous colors (page 29), as well as using a color's tint, tone, and shades (page 27). For a detailed discussion of color and how to use it, see Color (page 22).

Appealing repetition of windows in Portugal

Balance

Balance is achieved when the design elements are arranged to produce an aesthetically pleasing result. There are many types of balance including symmetrical (where the design elements are the same on both sides of an axis) and asymmetrical. While some facades are symmetrical, most of the quilts created using the techniques in this book will be asymmetrical.

To achieve a balanced asymmetrical design, an accepted convention used by artists and photographers is to divide the picture into nine sections—three vertically and three horizontally. This is known as the *rule of thirds*. The lines and points of intersection represent places to position important visual elements, such as the focal point (next page).

Designs include a balance of positive and negative space. Positive shapes are those of the actual image and the negative shapes are those around or in between objects. Together these two elements create a dynamic duet. Having negative space allows the positive shapes to shine and stand out. It will also provide a quieter place for the viewer's eyes to rest before returning to the focal point.

Fisherman's Bastion, Budapest by Pam Edwards, 20″ × 33″ (51 cm × 84 cm)

Blue negative space supports and showcases detail in stunning building.

TIP ~ Another good practice is to avoid stopping any shape just at the edge of your design—it's better to take a shape right off the edge than to have it just touch it. Also avoid having a shape or strong line leading toward a corner as this tends to lead the eye quickly out of the design.

Focal Point

The strongest part of a design is known as the *focal point* or *area of focus*. This is what commands the viewer's attention and has the strongest impact— all other areas should move toward it and support it. You can draw attention to the focal point in a number of different ways, one of the most powerful being a big jump in value. It is interesting that the eye sees value, the relative lightness or darkness of color, before it registers color. Value differences are therefore a powerful contrast and can certainly make a focal point stand out. So that other areas don't then compete, blend middle values as you move away from the focal point so they will not distract and draw attention elsewhere. Other contrasts that can be used include a strong splash of rich color, the use of complementary colors (page 28), or a gap in a pattern. An intersection of lines has the capacity to also become a focal point.

Looking at your image, place the strongest part of your design on one of the vertical thirds (see Balance, previous page). Aligning a subject with these points, rather than in the center, creates more tension, energy, and interest in the composition.

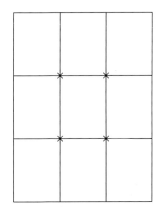

The eye is drawn to adjacent complementary colored buildings through archway.

Position focal point at one point of intersection.

If you have a horizon line, try to not cut the design in half by placing this in the center, but perhaps somewhere near the bottom third line.

Movement

When the eye of the viewer is drawn from one area to another and in particular to the focal point (page 15), the design will come alive. Make the journey as interesting as possible without providing an easy exit, such as a strong line leading straight out the side of the design. Repeated marks, lines, shapes, and colors can act as arrows to lead the viewer along an imaginary path.

Emphasizing horizontal lines and shapes will give the design a feeling of tranquility and peacefulness. The landscape can be made up of a series of horizontal lines including the distant horizon where the sky meets the ground, the calm sea, or the contours of the still desert.

In contrast, vertical lines are usually man-made and imply strength. Sometimes defying gravity, vertical lines add energy and almost an implied pride in attaining height. Some of the incredible modern skyscrapers are wonderful examples of this.

Vertical designs do not have to be actually perpendicular in the design. They can be more interesting if they are slightly angled.

Repetition of vertical fence rails creates movement across surface.

Strong vertical lines of skyscrapers, Dubai

Diagonal lines imply movement as they provide patterns of motion directing your eye. If well placed, a diagonal line sweeping across the composition, can grab the viewers' attention and take them on a visual journey to visit other areas of the design.

If you feel that your building does not provide an invitation to lead the viewer in for a visit, you may have to use the foreground to do this. The addition of diagonal movement can be created by using elements such as steps, a path or fence line to draw the viewer into the design.

Steps and handrail invite viewer into image in Geraldton, Western Australia.

Curved stairway draws the eye to red door in Montreal.

Contrast

It's important to strive for harmony, but if the elements are too similar in size, color, and value, you are in danger of creating an image that is boring and lacking in drama and excitement. There are many ways to push contrast while being careful not to overdo it resulting in chaos. The contrast between the two complementary colors (page 28), texture next to plain, dark next to light, warm next to cool, crisp edges next to organic edges, large shapes next to small, are all ways to add drama and energy to your work.

Changes of color and shape provide contrast in window shapes.

FINDING AN IMAGE

As you wander your local area or head off to more distant destinations, there is a wealth of fascinating and intriguing facades to use as inspiration for your quilt.

One of my favorite pastimes when traveling is to just wander with my camera, capturing images for later analysis. Freezing the subject in a photograph allows you the time to study and interpret the subject more accurately. Try to compose the image when looking through the viewfinder or on your smartphone screen. The camera frames the subject and helps make decisions such as whether to use a vertical or horizontal format. Take photographs using both formats so you can compare and decide later.

Taking a single photograph may not give you enough information. Take detailed shots and try taking photographs from different angles to give you a wonderful resource from which to build your design.

Same location, different views

In this wonderful technological age, your phone is usually in your pocket, giving you unlimited and constant access to a camera. But remember that photos are just the starting point. They will record the light, the actions, the place, and the people. It is what you do with this initial resource that is critical.

Cropping

An important consideration when planning the design is the distance from yourself to the subject. The further away you are, the less detail you will see. It does mean more building can be included but may also mean more foreground and sky depending on how you want to crop the picture.

Moving in closer to the subject reveals more detail, such as stonework, images in windows, doorways, and other architectural features—even extraordinary door handles, if you are really close.

Moving in close reveals astonishing door handle in Barcelona.

Original image cropped to highlight the detail of facade in Aveiro, Portugal

It can be very helpful to make a viewfinder to help you zero in on the essence of the subject. Your camera lens, L-shaped cardboard frames, or even your hands (using your thumbs and forefingers to complete a rectangle), can all be used as framing devices.

If the building itself is of importance and the context is of little interest, consider filling the entire area with it, omitting any background. On the other hand, if the setting is part of what attracted you to the image in the first place, then you have to make a decision about how much of it to include. A big area of boring background can have a major impact on an image—keep the background tight so that it enhances the subject rather than detracting from it.

Foreground provides sense of place.

Cropping plays such a critical role. Sometimes, when selecting just a slice of a building, the image moves from being realistic to wonderfully abstract, focusing on the interplay of pattern and color.

Stunning tall building in Melbourne

Cropping to give superb abstract pattern

Backgrounds

If you have decided to include some background in your design, think about how realistic and detailed it will be. Consider carefully what you are trying to achieve or what your pictures represent.

One approach is to create just a hint of a surrounding town or landscape. This can be done using a collage approach in which the detail is blurred as you manipulate shapes and colors.

The color of the sky is important, but the main emphasis should be that the sky color works well with the building. If sky and water are both featured in the same image, the water will take on the color of the sky but be a darker value.

Buildings are often used as the focal point in a larger scene. Their structure can lure the eye into picture so where you place them is very important. They can be used as a dominant feature to give a sense of scale or used as a contrast to the landscape such as reflections in water or rolling hills.

Foliage can be a good framing device with the soft, natural greens, providing a good contrast to the hard edges of buildings.

Photo by C&T Publishing

Dromana Boatsheds by Marnie Mascioli, 24″ × 12″ (60 cm × 30 cm)

Soft foliage frames strong lines of boat sheds.

Buildings on side of hill are framed by metal bridge in Porto, Portugal.

Scale

The addition of figures or fixtures, such as lampposts, benches, and letter boxes, create a sense of proportion and scale. The placement of figures is very important as they naturally draw the eye into the frame. It is crucial to position them on or near one of the third lines (see Balance, page 14), where they will balance the design of the image.

Positioning objects, such as a streetlight or bicycle in the foreground, also help create an illusion of depth.

Lamp in foreground adds to feeling of depth.

Light and Shadows

Lastly, the magic ingredient—light! Light brings everything to life. Look at how the light falls on the facade. Consider the direction the light is coming from and its effect on the surface of the facade. Which areas are brighter, and where have the shadows formed?

A shadow is an area of space screened from light and is never totally dark or black. Shadows can provide extra interest to the surface of our buildings, which tend to be flat shapes.

There are three types of shadows:

This archway creates areas of light and shade.

Dark line of shade appears where rocks touch each other.

- When the light is hitting the front of a structure, side walls are in shadow. This area of shadow will be a darker, less intense version of the original color.

- When an object such as a light pole blocks the light, a shadow is cast on the structure. Most sharply focused near their source, these shadows are darker, less intense versions of the color they fall upon. Toning down a color in the shadow by adding its complement is an effective approach if you want to add paint.

- There are also shadows where objects touch each other. The dark line around a closed door or the dark line around rocks making up a wall are known as *proximity shadows*. These shadows show us that the objects are separated.

Osaka Castle in the Shade by Carol McFadzean, 26″ × 37″
(66 cm × 94 cm)

For many of us, buildings are familiar subjects that we know and love. They reflect our history, our climate, and our lifestyle. From shopping malls to cathedrals, railway stations to sporting pavilions, boat sheds to art galleries, they are fascinating subjects to study and a wonderful inspiration for quilt designs.

View from bridge at Girona, Spain

Church of the Savior, St. Petersburg by Julie Hayes, 21½″ × 17″
(55 cm × 43 cm)

Il Duomo di Firenze by Danielle Hodge, 31″ × 22″ (79 cm × 56 cm)

COLOR

Old buildings lit up for Vivid Festival in Sydney

Sydney Opera House Vivid Festival by Gloria Loughman, 49″ × 32″ (122 cm × 81 cm)

An important part of the design process is to choose a color palette. You may decide to make a quilt in the original colors featured in your image. It may well be that these stunning colors were the feature that inspired you in the first place. Alternatively, it may be the facade of the building itself, rather than the color scheme that draws you in. If this is the case, use the facade as a starting point and color it in with a very different set of colors.

Colorful houses nestled on cliff top in Corniglia, Italy

Series of colorful doors, Porto, Portugal

Colorful buildings side by side on riverbank in Girona, Spain

COLOR AND CULTURE

The world is home to an astounding variety of cultures, many of whom who use bright color in a multitude of ways. Unlike the subtle variations of color and the neutrals favored on facades of buildings in many Western cultures, some of the buildings in countries such as Mexico, India, Central Africa, and South America are a paintbox of dazzling color. Painted shutters, doors, window frames, balconies, and verandah posts often clash happily with walls in outrageous colors. It seems that in some of the poorer areas of the world, where resources are limited, the sheer richness of color delights the soul.

Old traditional colored buildings line street in Bath, England.

Old and modern colorful houses side by side in Bristol, England

Vibrant bright colors of café in Portugal

On a recent visit to the historic fishing village of St. John's in Newfoundland, Canada, we were entranced by the incredible color palette of the row houses. The story goes that when sea captains returned from their voyages, they were faced with rows and rows of identical Victorian houses. In order to make these houses standout from one another, each house was painted a different vibrant color. The sailors could then find their way home quickly. This tradition continued on and as a result, Newfoundland is one of the most colorful and beautiful parts of Canada.

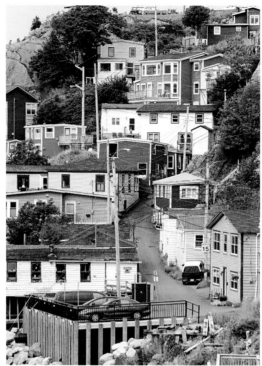

Colorful fishing village, St. John's, Canada

Houses painted bright colors in Burano, Italy

Likewise, in Italy, the Venetian island town of Burano could be the most colorful in the world. Legend has it that the fishermen painted their houses in bright luminous colors so that they could see them in thick fog and avoid crashing into the shore. They used ship's paint, which traditionally came in bright colors so that the boats were visible at sea, especially in fog. Since then, the Italian town has kept up the tradition and continues to paint its houses in a huge variety of different shades with no two houses next to each other the same.

THE ART OF COLOR

When alighting from the train in Riomaggiore, one of the five towns that make up Cinque Terre on the Italian coast, I was overwhelmed with delight and a burst of positive energy as I spun around, taking in the beautiful bold colors of the houses surrounding me. Color is such an emotive component—able to stimulate our emotions, uplift our spirits, and inspire us.

Stunning colored houses at Manorola, Italy

Bold colors of seaside village at Riomaggiore, Italy

Color sense starts with observation. Few people are born with an intuitive sense of color and most of us build up our knowledge and expertise like any other skill. Color is so much part of our lives and we can learn so much by looking around us, finding inspiration often from unexpected sources. Plants, spools of thread, tiles, industrial areas, buildings, recipe books, and, of course, the work of other artists.

Artists have a passion for color, some have even been obsessed with it. Study the work of artists such as Botticelli, Turner, Van Gogh, Matisse, Klee, Kandinsky, and Hundertwasser. These artists were focused on thoroughly exploring the potential of color, its characteristics, and mood.

Cool colors, spools of wool at the Victorian Tapestry museum

Spools of wool in warm colors

Cool colored tiles

Warm colored tiles on a stairway in San Francisco

COLOR COMBINATIONS

From appreciating colors in all their richness and beauty, it is a short step to exploring the endless variety of color combinations on offer to us. The harmonious families, in which each color blends and supports each other; the electric mixes, where the color resonates; or simple graphic contrasts are all combinations that you can explore and use in your work. Having the knowledge of which colors are members of a family that will harmonize naturally, which colors vibrate and sing, and why some combinations don't work at all, can be of wonderful assistance and help you to create exciting and vibrant color schemes.

The Color Wheel

A good way to get an understanding of color combinations is to begin with the color wheel. Historically, there have been different color wheels developed that artists have used as a guide for mixing colors. Many artists use the twelve-color wheel of Johannes Itten, which was the reference tool for the color section in my previous books. In this book, you'll see the Ives color wheel, which is based on using yellow, cyan, and magenta as the primary colors that can be mixed to make all other colors—cyan is a beautiful blue, a touch on the green side; magenta is rich red that is a touch on the blue side.

These are the colors of the ink used to print on paper (think books, magazines, and so on) and the color of dyes, paints, and pigments used for coloring fabrics. (Try experimenting with fabric paints using these as the starting colors—you will find that you get some beautiful hues.)

Mix two primary colors together to get the secondary colors of green (yellow + cyan), orange (yellow + magenta), and violet (cyan + magenta). The tertiary colors, which comprise the rest of the colors on the wheel, result from mixing the primary colors with secondary colors.

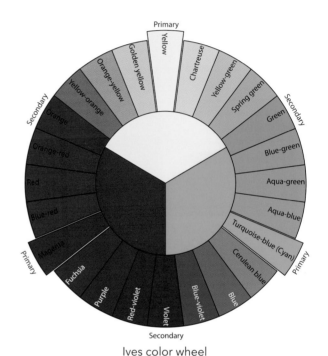

Ives color wheel

Pure Colors

The colors on this wheel are the pure colors and some combination of the three primaries of yellow, cyan, and magenta. Each of these pure colors has its own color family, which is made up of its tints, shades, and tones.

A color is at its most saturated when it is pure, with no added black or white. Pure colors provide drama and excitement. Yellow is the lightest pure color and purple is the darkest.

Tints

Pure colors become a tint when white is added. When mixing paint to create paler colors, always start with white and gradually add the color.

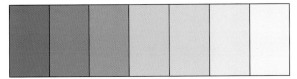

Tints from blue-violet family

Shades

Pure colors become a shade when black is added. Shades that are on the warm side of the color wheel not only become darker but also change color. Yellow becomes olive green, yellow-orange becomes brown, orange becomes rust. In comparison, on the cooler side of the wheel, violet becomes dark violet, blue becomes dark blue.

Shades from orange family

Tone

If gray is added to a pure color, a tint, or a shade it is known as a tone. When a small amount of gray is added, the color becomes more muted. If a lot of gray is added it can be difficult to work out the original color, but the gray will have a particular feel such as a pinkish gray or greenish gray. When looking at ranges of fabric consider which family of grays will work with your other colors.

Tones of gray in violet family

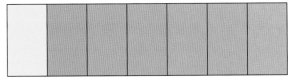

Tones of gray in yellow family

Warm and Cool Colors

The color wheel divides naturally in to a warm side and a cool side. Red, orange, and yellow are generally considered to be warm. Green, blue, and violet form the cool side. Hues that appear to have more yellow in them are warm, while those with more blue are cooler.

The temperature of any color is actually dependent on the colors placed next to it—in other words, color temperature can be altered by adjacent colors. A hue that appears warm when it stands alone may become cool when surrounded by warm tones.

Purple looks warm next to blue.

Same purple looks cool next to red-orange.

The size and placement of color areas also affect the impact of temperature. A small spot of yellow-orange within a large area of a cool color, such as cerulean blue, will have more zing than equally sized areas of warm and cool hues. The amount of bright yellow-orange stands out and demands attention.

Small amount of yellow-orange stands out

Impact is reduced when amount of yellow-orange color is increased.

Color choices tend to set the mood of the design. Warm colors are alive and energetic; they can project light and happiness. Cooler colors are more restful and at times more mysterious. They can portray a feeling of serenity and calmness.

Color Schemes

Monochromatic

A monochromatic color scheme is based on a single color family. The pure color, plus a number of its tints, shades, and tones can be used. Although it is the simplest color scheme, I have found it to be one of the most difficult to use. It is a wonderful challenge and I would encourage every quilt artist, who wants to improve her use of color, to make a mono-chromatic quilt. It is important to include a range from light to dark and if possible, contrasting textures. I have found it difficult to find enough fabrics in one family to give me the range I need, so it has been back to the dye bath creating the fabric myself.

Seaside Cottage color sample by Marnie Mascioli, 10″ × 18″ (25 cm × 46 cm)

Made using monochromatic warm colors

Seaside Cottage color sample by Donna M. MacDonald, 10″ × 18″ (25 cm × 46 cm)

Made using monochromatic cool colors

Working with a monochromatic color scheme forces you to concentrate on using value to create contrast. When done successfully, the work is striking and dramatic.

Complementary

This dynamic and exciting color scheme is based on using two color families that are opposite each other on the color wheel. When positioned side by side, the colors appear to vibrate off each other, enhancing their brilliance.

When two complementary colors are mixed together, they produce a fabulous range of muddy or neutral colors. A variety of these muddy/neutral colors juxtaposed with small amounts of pure color is a striking and very effective color scheme.

Hand-dyed fabric using yellow and violet dye

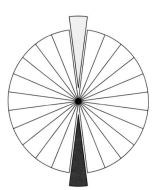

Complementary colors

Another alternative is to vary this color scheme by using the color next to the complement. Instead of using yellow and violet, try yellow and blue-violet or yellow and red-violet for stunning results.

Successful color combinations often depend on getting the proportions right. A touch of contrasting color is lively and refreshing; too much can be uncomfortable if blocks of complementary colors are competing for attention. Make one color family the main color and the other the accent for a more vibrant and powerful effect. This helps give movement to the work as the eye will move across the work, connecting the accents.

Detail of old locomotive, showing highlight of red on green background

Complementary color scheme of pink art deco house with green water feature in Porto, Portugal

Seaside Cottage color sample by Gloria Loughman, 10″ × 18″ (25 cm × 46 cm)

Made using complementary color scheme of purple with yellow-green.

Los Gatos Medical Center by Barbara Serwitz, 25″ × 38½″ (64 cm × 98 cm)

This quilt uses a complementary color scheme of blue and orange.

Analogous

Always a favorite, the analogous color scheme is made up of color families next to each other on the color wheel. These colors blend naturally with each other, with the flow from one color to the next being an easy progression that does not impact on the properties of each individual color.

Often seen in nature, this harmonious color scheme is probably the easiest to use. If you are using the Ives color wheel (page 26) try using five or more colors that are next to each other for a beautiful effect. You can continue around the wheel using almost half the wheel but stopping when you get to the complement.

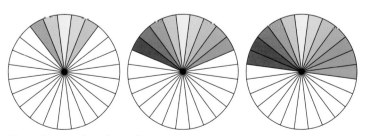

Five, nine, and twelve colors

It can be helpful to choose some fabrics that showcase more than one color to bring further harmony to your work.

If you don't know where to begin, choose a color on the wheel you want to feature then add two or more colors that are on either side of this original color.

Old bank Building, Kilmore by Gloria Loughman, 22½˝ × 32˝ (57 cm × 81 cm)

Another warm, analogous color scheme

Seaside Cottage color sample by Donna M. MacDonald, 10˝ × 18˝ (25 cm × 46 cm)

Made using analogous color scheme of yellow, golden yellow, orange-yellow, yellow-orange, and orange

Photo by Neil Porter

Artisan's House by Jill Exell, 11˝ × 31½˝ (28 cm × 80 cm)

Made using warm, analogous color scheme

Split Complementary

This color scheme is made up of a group of color families adjacent to each other on the color wheel plus a wonderful accent with the addition of the complement from the other side. It is harmonious yet spectacular and eye-catching. The adjacent families of color set the mood and the complement provides the magical ingredient that makes the quilt come alive.

Split-complementary color schemes

The number of adjacent colors can vary from three to seven. If you work with a large number of adjacent colors, try increasing the complementary colors to three, remembering that they are still an accent and thus need to be in smaller proportion.

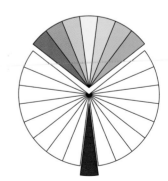

Extended split-complementary color scheme

Seaside Cottage color sample by Gloria Loughman, 10″ × 18″ (25 cm × 46 cm)

Made using split-complementary color scheme of violets, reds, and orange with spring green accent.

Seaside Cottage color sample by Donna M. MacDonald, 10″ × 18″ (25 cm × 46 cm)

Made using yellow to orange with aqua-green complement

Facades in Perspective by Jane Grove, 20″ × 18″ (51 cm × 46 cm)

Jane used split-complementary color scheme of orange and yellow with a blue accent.

Triadic

Triadic color schemes are based on the fact that there is a special relationship between colors that are equal distance apart on the color wheel. These colors are a long way apart and form a triangle. This color scheme provides high contrast, variety, and impact yet still retains harmony.

If the colors chosen seem to be overwhelming or even gaudy, try using tints, shades, and toned-down triadic colors to create a vibrant and beautiful effect.

There are eight possible triadic color combinations on the Ives color wheel:

- Yellow, cyan, and magenta
- Chartreuse, cerulean blue, and blue-red (one of my favorites)
- Yellow-green, blue, and red
- Spring green, blue-violet, and orange-red
- Green, violet, and orange
- Blue-green, red-violet, and yellow-orange
- Aqua-green, purple, and orange-yellow
- Aqua-blue, fuchsia, and golden yellow (another favorite)

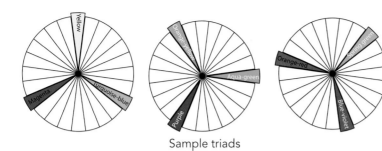

Sample triads

When using a triadic scheme, one color family should be the visually dominant color, with the second color taking on a lesser role, and the third color just an accent. As the colors are a long distance from each other on the color wheel, you have to work hard to make them relate to each other and create some harmony. Try to include at least one or more fabrics that have more than one of the corresponding triad colors in them to help them to blend.

This is a color scheme that I might never have tried, except as an exercise, but it has become one of my favorites, as it is more edgy and not as predictable.

Seaside Cottage color sample by Gloria Loughman, 10″ × 18″ (25 cm × 46 cm)

Made using the triad of chartreuse, cerulean blue, and red-blue

Black, White, and Gray with One Color

This final color scheme is full of drama and one that is often used in advertising, as it is so eye-catching. Guilds often challenge their members to make a quilt in this color scheme. Although you have limited yourself to one color, you have the option of using tints, shades, and tones to get more variation. Think carefully about the placement of the sections of color. It may be that the image is mainly black and white with just some accents in color.

Moody Busselton by Sue Pope, 41½″ × 19″ (105 cm × 48 cm)

This quilt features color scheme of black, white, and gray with aqua-blue for moody feel.

Seaside Cottage color sample by Donna M. MacDonald, 10″ × 18″ (25 cm × 46 cm)

Made using black, white, gray with yellow-orange

COLOR BALANCE

After you have chosen the color scheme, you have to decide on the placement of each color as you strive for balance. Start by deciding which color family will be dominant and which colors will be the accents. An effective approach, used in interior design, is to use the ratio 60/30/10 for a three-color palette. The dominant color will cover the most area (60%) while the accent colors (30% and 10%) complement and balance out that main color. Think about how the colors look when side by side. Do they blend where you don't want too much contrast, or alternatively, do they contrast enough to draw the eye to the focal point (page 15)?

It is sometimes easier to achieve balance when you don't have too many colors. Try adding shades and tints to expand your color choices without overwhelming the image with a kaleidoscope of colors.

Melbourne Exhibition Building by Marion Davidson, 21˝ × 24˝ (53 cm × 61 cm)

Basic color palette is extended by using shades and tints.

WORKING WITH THE ORIGINAL COLOR SCHEME

If you have decided to use the original color scheme for inspiration, you can still make changes to make the work more exciting and dramatic. Try changing the tone, tints, and shades, to add more contrast. Experiment with different background colors to make the image more eye-catching.

Original photo of Old Town, Yellowknife, Canada

Old Town, Yellowknife by Gloria Loughman, 23″ × 32″
(58 cm × 81 cm)

Dramatic color scheme of original inspiration photo resulted in dynamic quilt with just a few changes.

COLOR AND PERSPECTIVE

You can use color temperatures to create depth or distance in your design. Cooler colors tend to recede while warmer colors appear to be closer to the front of a design. Colors also become more muted as they move into the distance. Colors in the foreground are richer and more saturated. Don't be afraid to use strong values in your work to draw attention to the focal point and create drama.

Finally, it is important for you to develop your own eye for color. For those fortunate few who have an innate sense of color, we applaud and envy you. For the rest of us, we can succeed by analyzing the work of other artists, exploring nature and the landscape, photographing urban vistas, and sourcing beautiful fabrics. Play with colors, experiment! It is a wonderful journey!

Colors of buildings fade off into distance.

Notice how warm colors appear to move forward.

Doc by the Tankstand by Jeannie Henry,
16″ × 20″ (41 cm × 51 cm)

Warm color on tank seems to move
forward in this quilt.

FABRIC

Camping in My Other Kombi by Gloria Loughman, 17″ × 26″ (43 cm × 66 cm)

For instructions, see *Campervan*, page 115.

With so many amazing commercial and hand-produced fabric available, it is sometimes hard to know where to start when selecting fabric. The fabric samples shown in this book are cotton, but the selection could include silk, polyester, home decor fabrics, or any other fabric that works well for texture and color and isn't too thick to work with.

DARK FABRICS FOR THE BASE

Each of the main pieces of the facade will be constructed on its own dark base. The ideal fabric for the bases is one with a high thread count, such as batik. Later in the construction process, this base will be trimmed back so only ⅛″ (3 mm) is showing around the visible edges. A fabric that has a looser weave will tend to fray. Also, choose a fabric that has the same or similar color on the front and back. If a black fabric that is cream on the back is used, when the edge is trimmed, it is likely a cream line will stand out.

So choose your fabric carefully for the bases. The fabric can be a plain black or have a small pattern on a very dark background. Basically you want the dark color to read as a continuous line around the edge of the shapes. A dark hand-dyed fabric, with a high thread count, will also work well.

Dark base fabrics

If you have a particular color scheme in mind for the facade, you can match this to the dark base so that they are in the same family. Alternatively, consider choosing the complementary color (page 28) to give more contrast. An example would be a dark teal base fabric as a contrast for a facade that features the orange family.

FABRICS FOR WALLS

There are so many options for the walls. Look at your image. Should the walls feature a plain fabric, such as those shown below? Some gorgeous fabrics that just have subtle texture work so beautifully on walls and trims.

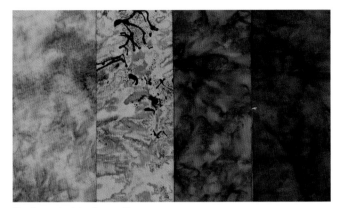

Batiks suitable for walls

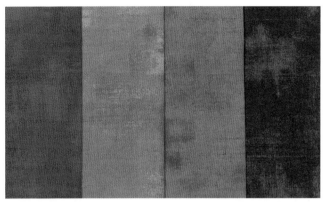

Beautiful, shaded tone on tones

A range of fabric that I love using to create older, more textured facades are those from the Ananse Village (anansevillage.com). These fabrics, created in Ghana, are often printed onto damask, a very textured fabric. Profits from the sale of these fabrics are shared with the communities that produce them.

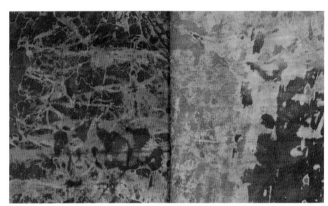

Fabrics produced in Ghana

For a more abstract feel to the facade, you can find fabulous commercial fabrics with geometric prints and patterns.

In recent times companies have produced ranges of fabric that have the appearance of rock. These are wonderful for rock walls and old crumbling plaster.

Use geometric patterns for abstract look.

Rock textures

FABRICS FOR TRIMS

Often plainer fabrics work well when the piece is quite narrow, such as a window frame, and the line needs to be distinct.

Fabrics with hint of texture

FABRICS FOR GLASS

Fabrics that feature tone on tone, blurry images, or have a transparent feel work well to mimic glass.

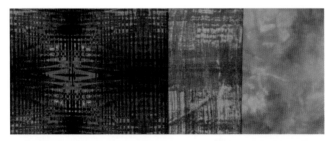

Various fabrics that mimic glass

FABRICS FOR SKY

If you have included an area of sky in the design, then you have a lot of fabric options to consider. You can find commercial fabrics that look like the striations in the sky. Alternatively, you can paint the sky on a piece of white fabric. If perspective is not important and you just want a great negative space around the facade, consider a plainer, hand-dyed fabric or commercial fabric to give you the contrast you are chasing.

Batik fabric suitable as sky

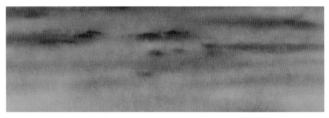

Hand-painted sky fabric

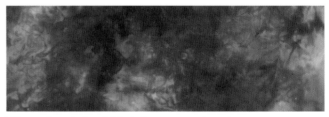

Vibrant hand-dyed fabric for contrasting sky

Commercial fabric suitable for contrasting sky

TIP My other books—*Radiant Landscapes*, *Quilted Symphony*, and *Luminous Landscapes* (all from C&T Publishing)—feature sections on painting and dyeing your own fabric, perfect for unique skies.

FABRICS FOR FOREGROUND AND WATER

Fabrics that have horizontal lines are often a good choice for areas of foreground and water.

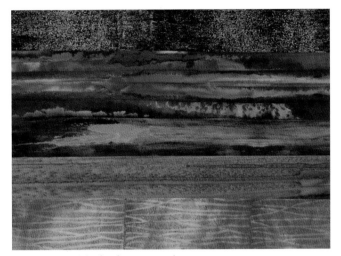

Fabrics suitable for foregrounds

OVERPAINTING COMMERCIAL FABRICS

A number of excellent commercial fabrics available mimic bricks, stone walls, tree trunks, and other textures. If the scale of the print works for your design, you can even overpaint these to fit in with your color palette. A light wash using diluted fabric paint or even soft-body artist's acrylic paint might be all you need.

Commercial fabrics with small scale bricks that can be overpainted

Small Town Merchant by B. Jan Gavin, 23½″ × 32″ (60 cm × 81 cm)

Different shades of overpainted commercial brick fabric are used to create perspective.

Fireweed Studio by Hazel Wainwright, 28″ × 24″ (71 cm × 61 cm)

Commercial fabrics provide wonderful texture for cabin walls.

CREATING TEXTURED FABRICS

A number of quilt artists create their own beautiful, unique fabrics using screen printing, stamping, and stenciling techniques. A lot of wonderful, informative books have been written on mastering these techniques. A good book to refer to is *Create Your Own Hand-Printed Cloth* by Rayna Gillman (from C&T Publishing).

Hand-painted and stenciled fabrics work well on walls and doors.

Another process that creates a wonderful distressed surface on fabric is to add painted fusible web. Double-sided fusible web, such as Wonder-Under, can be painted with diluted acrylic paint. When the fusible is dry, cut it in to shapes and, using silicone release paper or baking parchment, carefully press it to the surface of the fabric. Metallic paints in particular look amazing when applied to dark surfaces. As the web is quite fragile, secure it to the fabric with stitching to increase resilience.

Detail of *Time Reveals* (page 76) by Suzann Moss. Painted fusible web on surface of doorway

STEPS TO PREVENT FRAYING

As well as choosing fabrics that have a high thread count, an option is to use a product such as Terial Magic (by Terial Arts)— a spray product that is marketed as a no-fray spray stabilizer. Spray the Terial Magic on the fabric, wring it out, and allow it to dry. After pressing, the fabric feels like paper and the edges can be cut smoothly with either a rotary cutter or scissors. This is especially handy if you are cutting very narrow window frames or delicate features to add to the facade.

The techniques in this book use repositionable paper-packed fusible web, such as Lite Steam-A-Seam 2, to layer and secure fabric pieces. If a piece in question does not already have fusible web on it, pressing fusible web before cutting will help support the edge and minimize fraying.

Eureka Graffiti by Charli Bakker, 19½″ × 39½″ (50 cm × 100 cm)

Wonderful walls covered in graffiti drawn on white fabric.

creating THE PATTERN

Federation Style, Geelong by Gloria Loughman, 26″ × 24″ (66 cm × 61 cm)

After you have selected the image and made any adjustments, such as cropping (page 18) and editing (page 13), it is time to create the design full-size on paper. This will become the pattern that you will refer to many times throughout the process of constructing the quilt.

If the thought of drawing out a design is too daunting, you can skip ahead to Photocopying and Using Your Computer (page 48) for a number of other ways to create your design, but I do encourage you to try drawing a design at least once; you might find that you rather enjoy it.

DRAWING THE DESIGN

When drawing your design, it is important that you follow the rules of perspective and make sure things are in proportion. It may be a good idea to do a number of small sketches first to work out the main shapes and lines.

When you look at a photograph, you can easily get bogged down with the details. Start by mapping out the larger shapes first, especially in relation to the sky and ground. Also keep in mind that the farther away the buildings are, the less detail they need.

The most straightforward image to use for a pattern is a photograph that has been taken straight on. With this view, you can concentrate on the fabrics and colors to create interest and perspective, without the hassle of dealing with vanishing points.

French Quarter by Jennifer Corkish, 33″ × 15½″ (84 cm × 39 cm)

Straight-on view highlights beautiful color scheme and detail in shutters.

Mum's House by Janice Hughes, 28″ × 19″ (71 cm × 48 cm)

Straight-on view allows for a lot of wonderful detail

Using Perspective

There are two types of perspective: aerial and linear.

Aerial perspective is based on creating an illusion of depth through fabric choice—as parts of the building move back in to the distance, the colors will be more faded, cooler, and less textured.

Linear perspective is used by artists to determine the relative size, shape, and position of objects, using drawn or imagined lines that converge at a vanishing point or points.

It is important that both types of perspective are successfully managed to give you a pleasing result.

Creating the illusion of depth on a flat piece of paper may seem like a magic trick, but linear perspective depends on following rules that are very easy to master.

One-Point Perspective

This is the simplest type of perspective as it deals with just one side of the building that moves toward the background.

Inspirational photo—facade receding into distance

1. Establish where the horizon is positioned—this is where the sky meets the land. If you can't see the horizon because the building is in the way, assume a position for the horizon about a third of the way up in the image. Draw this line across a copy of the image, making sure it is straight and horizontal.

Draw horizon.

2. Draw in a vertical line representing the closest part or corner of the building.

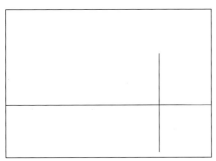

Draw closest vertical line.

3. Look at the building, noting in particular the line of the roof, the top of the window frames, the top of the door, and the bottom edge. As these lines head toward the horizon, they will either angle up or down, depending on whether they are above or below the horizon. If they are positioned above the horizon they will angle down, and if they are below they will angle up toward it.

4. In one-point perspective, all these lines should converge to the same point on the horizon. This is called the *vanishing point*. All the buildings in the image facing the same way and on the same level will have the same vanishing point. Study the image to establish the position of this point. Drawing is about interpretation and not technical accuracy, so as long as your drawing looks believable, then the drawing is successful. Sometimes this vanishing point will be positioned out of your design, but since it is a critical reference point, take time to establish where it is positioned.

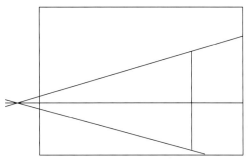

Lines converge to vanishing point.

5. Add the windows and doors—make a mark to establish the top and bottom corners of the nearest doors and windows, and then draw a faint line through to the vanishing point. Using this line as a reference, draw in the windows and doors, including those further in the distance.

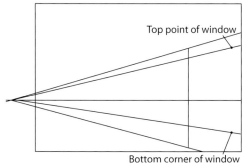

Top point of window

Bottom corner of window

Mark nearest top and bottom corner of windows and door and draw faint line through vanishing point.

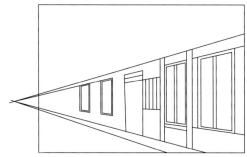

Draw in windows and doors using this line as reference.

The side of a building will appear to get smaller as it recedes toward the vanishing point. When you are happy with the first building, you can start to put in more details including other buildings, if they are relevant to the design.

TIP For most designs, it's important to keep the vertical lines straight. If they slant, even a little, it will appear as if the building is leaning over.

Fabulous Facade Francais by Anne Hunt, 32½″ × 21½″ (83 cm × 55 cm)

Notice how side of building recedes.

Two-Point Perspective

Two-point perspective enables you to draw two sides of a building and have them both recede into the distance.

It is drawn the same way as the one-point perspective, except you do it on both sides of the facade.

1. Draw the horizon line and the closet vertical corner. This will indicate the height of the building.

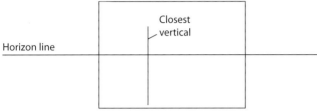

Horizon line and closest vertical

2. When you have established these two lines, refer to the photograph to establish two vanishing points, one on each side of the vertical corner line.

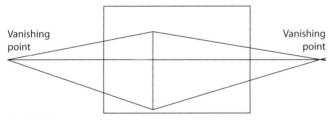

Establish two vanishing points.

TIP If the vanishing points are off the piece of paper, just add more paper as needed.

3. Draw lines from the top and the bottom of the vertical line to the two vanishing points.

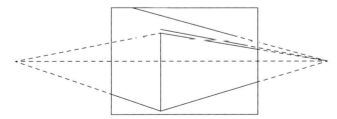

Add roof and base line of building.

Inspirational image where both walls recede

4. Draw the other vertical edges of the building. The position of these lines will be determined by the width of the walls.

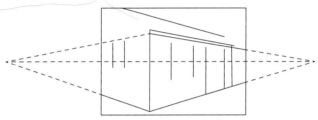

Add more vertical lines.

5. Draw in the windows, doors, and roof lines.

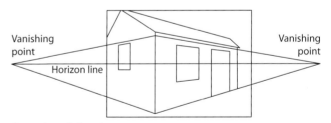

Completed drawing

TIP Remember that the rules of perspective apply to everything, including smaller details such as chimneys, fences, steps, and pathways.

Three-Point Perspective

Tall buildings, such as skyscrapers, appear to get narrower as they head toward the sky. The taller the building, the more it seems to converge. It may be that this merging shape is a feature of your design, but you do have the option of making these lines vertical, thus giving a different view of the building.

When drawing tall buildings, you need to use a third vanishing point.

1. Begin as you would with a two vanishing points, but before putting in the second and third vertical lines, place a third vanishing point above the first vertical. Project the second and third verticals up to this vanishing point, and then you will see the illusion of lines converging as they head toward the sky.

2. Project the other lines to the vanishing points on the horizon as for the two-dimensional perspective. The taller the building, the higher the vanishing point.

Edges of skyscrapers seem to converge.

New York skyline where buildings appear to get narrower.

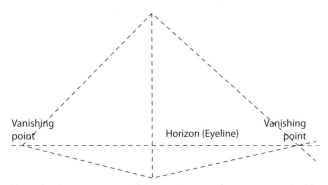

Draw horizon, two vanishing points, and nearest vertical line.

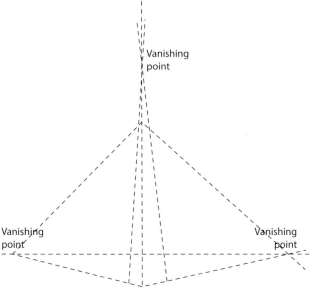

Add third vanishing point and second and third vertical lines.

The rules of perspective are fairly straightforward and if you draw a line at the wrong angle, this mistake will make the image feel unsettled. When you have drawn in the main outline, step back to see if the lines look correct. An eraser can come in very handy at this stage.

TIP Remember that vanishing points may converge off the drawing surface, especially if the angle of the building is small.

Italianate Facades by Susan Costantino, 29½″ × 27″ (75 cm × 69 cm)

Converging lines lead eye upward, giving height to building.

PHOTOCOPYING AND USING YOUR COMPUTER

If you prefer not to draw out the facade, you can create the pattern in other ways.

Photocopying and Tracing

If you are using one of your own photos, go to a copy shop and have it copied in black and white, and then enlarged and printed in the preferred size. To make the pattern, all you need is a clear black-and-white image that you can use to trace the main lines.

Source a good quality tracing paper, one robust enough to be used many times throughout the construction process. Vellum or drafting vellum is a good choice. It's available in art supply stores, some large office supply stores, stores that sell drafting supplies, and online. I use 29-pound (110 gsm) vellum.

Look at the large shapes first, tracing the key lines. Then go back in and add the details. Remember to simplify!

Original image of a public toilet block in Geraldton, Western Australia

Black-and-white photocopy at selected size

Tracing of building, including background to be included

Using Apps

You may use software programs, such as Photoshop and Photoshop Elements (by Adobe), on your computer to convert an original photograph to a line drawing. This is easy to do using the available filters.

Another option is to use an app. I use one for a smartphone or tablet called Sketch Guru (by Softonic). It is free to download and extremely simple to operate. I have found this to be a wonderful tool to assist me in converting my original photos into simple line drawings.

Original photo of old seaside cottage

1. Crop the original photo (see Cropping, page 18).

2. Select an option to convert the photo to a black-and-white line drawing (there are several—try them and use the one you like the best). I save this drawing to my photo gallery on my smartphone or tablet, and then email it to my copy center. I request them to print this line drawing at my specified size.

When I have the line drawing enlarged to my requested size, I use a lightbox to trace the key lines onto a large sheet of tracing paper. This becomes my pattern, which I will refer to many times during the construction process.

Cropped line drawing using Sketch Guru

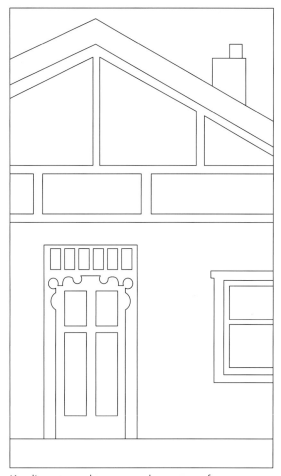

Key lines traced to create the pattern for *Seaside Cottage*

Outline Details on Tracing Paper

The final task before starting the construction process is to outline on the tracing paper the other details, so that they can be seen easily from the reverse side of the tracing-paper pattern. Use a fine-point Sharpie to outline the other elements you want to include, such as window frames, steps, and other decorative elements.

CONSTRUCTION

In Creating the Pattern (page 42) you learned how to prepare a tracing-paper pattern. Now it is time to learn about constructing the quilt. Basic to the process is that each wall and key element is constructed on its own dark base fabric. Edges that are visible in the final design are trimmed back to leave a fine dark line of the base fabric around each shape. Edges that tuck under are left untrimmed. Elements such as windows can be added to the wall and most of the stitching is completed before the building is appliquéd directly onto the sandwich.

In this chapter the basic construction process is explained as well as creating a few special facade surfaces.

Basic Construction Notes

Fusible web   Use a repositionable paper-backed fusible web such as Lite Steam-A-Seam 2. This allows you to adjust the positions of the pieces to get them placed just right before fusing them permanently in place.

Batting   Choose a thin dense batting, such as cotton or bamboo. If there is a scrim, face the scrim side down (otherwise it will melt when you press it. A thin fusible batting can also work—press the glue side to the backing fabric. You may spray baste the batting to the backing or pin with safety pins.

Needles and threads   A 40- or 50-weight thread will work well for most pieces. For narrow pieces, such as window frames, use a fine 60/8 or 70/10 needle and a fine 100-weight thread. I suggest a topstitch 80/12 needle for 40-weight thread, a topstitch 70/10 needle for 50-weight thread, and a microtex 60/8 needle for 60- to 100-weight thread.

Remember: For thread, the higher the number, the finer the thread. But for needles, the higher the number, the thicker the needle.

PREPARING FREEZER-PAPER PATTERNS FOR BASES

After you have made the tracing-paper pattern from a design you have drawn yourself or one from this book, decide how to split up the design into separate segments for construction. Each segment is constructed separately and then raw-edge appliquéd on a sandwich of batting and backing. Segments of sky, walls, roof, foreground, large doors, and so on are constructed individually.

1. On the tracing-paper pattern, draw over the outline of the main segments with a Sharpie, ignoring the details.

2. Decide which wall or piece will be positioned first on the batting when the various segments are appliquéd to the batting in sequence. Number these pieces, according to the order they will be applied to the batting. If there is a sky, it will be number 1, as it will be the first piece to be applied to the batting. Number 2 will be the next piece that is the furthest back in the design. Gradually work toward the front of the pattern, numbering as you go.

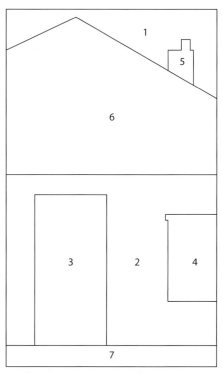

Outline major segments for construction. Add numbers, starting at back of design.

3. Place freezer paper dull side up on top of the tracing-paper pattern and trace the lines you drew with a Sharpie in Step 1 (previous page). Consider which segments are the basic structures and which details, such as doors and decorative elements, will be added later.

TIP To help you trace accurately, you may find it helpful to tape the tracing-paper drawing to the freezer paper and the table.

4. Name the freezer-paper pieces and number them according to their order of placement.

SEASIDE COTTAGE

BONUS DOWNLOAD You can make your own *Seaside Cottage* while you learn the basic techniques. To download the *Seaside Cottage* pattern, see How to Use This Book (page 6). Then print it out at home on 8½″ × 11″ (A4) paper and tile it together.

For information about drawing out designs on tracing paper, see Creating the Pattern (page 42) and Preparing Freezer-Paper Patterns for Bases (previous page).

Prepare the Base Pieces

1. Cut out the freezer-paper pattern pieces and press them onto the right side of the dark base fabric. The freezer paper should be dull side up, positioned with a 1″ (2.5 cm) space between each shape. Put to one side any sky or other background pieces, as these will be decided on and added later in the process.

2. After these shapes have been pressed in place with a hot iron, cut around each one with a generous ½″ (1.3 cm) margin for under/overlap.

3. Using a good quality chalk pencil, draw a fine line around each freezer-paper shape, ⅛″ (3 mm) out from the edge of the freezer paper.

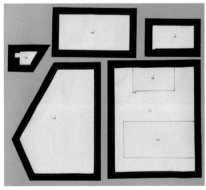

Draw chalk line ⅛″ (3 mm) outside edge of freezer paper.

4. Remove the freezer paper.

Seaside Cottage by Gloria Loughman, 10″ × 18″ (25 cm × 46 cm)

Add Fabric

1. After the bases are prepared, audition the fabric for the different pieces of the facade. One approach is to replicate the colors in an original photograph (see Working with the Original Color Scheme, page 34) or you can use a completely different color scheme (see Color, page 22). Consider using fabrics with textures and patterns to take advantage of the compelling and eye-catching contrast of plain fabric next to textured fabric.

Audition fabrics.

2. Trace each element from the back of the tracing-paper pattern onto the smooth side of repositionable paper-backed fusible web. After you have traced the image, add a ¼″ (6 mm) margin for under/overlap on any edge that will be tucked under or go in to the border.

3. Cut out the shape drawn on the fusible web leaving a small margin around the edge. Press the fusible web to the back of the selected fabrics. Cut out the fused fabric on the line including the under/overlap margin where necessary.

4. Peel off the backing paper from the fusible web and position the shapes on the corresponding base inside the chalk line, leaving ⅛″ (3 mm) margin around the edge. Edges that will be tucked under the adjacent shape or will go into the border will extend over the chalk line.

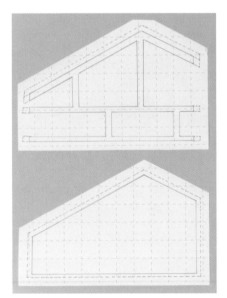

Add ¼″ (6 mm) margin for under/overlap as needed.

Cut shapes from fabric to assemble roof.

Assemble roof.

5. Prepare additional pieces from the tracing-paper pattern using the selected fabrics and fusible web.

Prepare pieces to make door.

Prepare pieces to make window.

Fuse door and window to base.

Make the Main Wall

Many cottages have siding/cladding or weatherboards, and there is a simple way to create this effect in fabric. Following the instructions in Add Fabric (page 52), cut the fabric for the siding wall, adding an under/overlap on all 4 edges.

1. Cut boards with a rotary cutter at the chosen width. For this design, the boards were cut ⅝˝ (1.6 cm) wide.

2. Peel off the fusible web backing paper and position these boards on the wall base, leaving a small gap in between each board. These boards need to be positioned over the chalk line, as adjacent shapes will cover the top and bottom edges, and the side edges will go out in to the border.

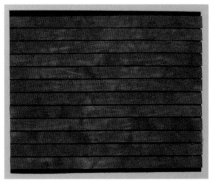

Position boards on wall base.

Add Stitching

After the roof, chimney, wall, door, and window have been constructed, it's time to stitch. The wonderful advantage of working on small segments is that they can be stitched before being appliquéd together. Detailed stitching around small windowpanes, fretwork, verandah posts, stone walls, and intricate doorways can be managed easily on the small segments.

TIP ⌒ This can be a good time to use decorative stitches that you may have on your sewing machine. A straight stitch is suitable for holding pieces in position, but decorative stitches are great for adding detail.

Stitch around all the elements in either a matching, variegated, or contrasting thread, depending on the design. For needle and thread recommendations, see Basic Construction Notes (page 50).

Add Background and Foreground

It is now time to choose the fabrics for the sky and foreground. Choose a fabric that works well with the building colors. For information on choosing sky fabric and other effects that can be used, see Fabrics for Sky (page 38).

The sky (segment 1) is the first segment to be positioned on the batting and does not need to be fused to a dark base. Press the freezer-paper pattern to the front of the sky fabric and cut it out with a generous ½˝ (1.3 cm) seam allowance.

The foreground (segment 7) *does* need a dark base, as it is the final piece to be added. Construct and stitch this segment, following the sections above for preparing the base (page 50), adding the fabric (page 52), making the main wall (page 53), and adding stitching (page 53) for the building segments.

Prepare sky and foreground segments.

Make the Quilt Sandwich

Because you build the quilt top directly on the batting and backing, the quilt sandwich is prepared earlier in the process than with other techniques.

At this point you need to consider how you will finish the quilt. If you are planning to add borders, cut the batting and backing with a 3˝ (8 cm) extra margin around the outside. If you have decided to finish the quilt with a narrow binding or facing, cut the batting and backing with an extra 1˝ (2.5 cm) margin around the outside of the pattern. If you aren't sure, include enough batting and backing that you can cut away if you opt for just a binding or facing.

Make the sandwich by pinning the batting and backing together with either straight pins or safety pins. *Note: Remember to remove the pins as you add fabric on top.*

Put It Together

1. After all the segments have been constructed and stitched, prepare the quilt sandwich. For this example, cut the batting and backing fabric, allowing a 1˝ (2.5 cm) margin around the edge of the pattern.

2. Place the tracing-paper design on the batting, marking the corners for quick placement. The tracing paper will be used as a guide for accurate placement of the segments.

3. Position the sky segment on the batting, checking the placement with the tracing-paper overlay. Pin it in position.

Use tracing-paper pattern to check sky placement.

4. Add the wall segment—to avoid bulk, the wall behind the doorway and window can be cut out. To do this, press the freezer-paper pattern of the door and window in position on the wall. Check for accurate placement using the tracing paper as an overlay. Draw a chalk line around the edge and then remove the freezer paper. Cut out the underneath piece, leaving a ¼˝ (6 mm) underlap.

Press freezer-paper patterns to wall as guide.

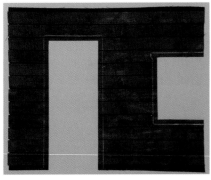

Cut out doorway and window to prevent bulk.

5. Press a 1˝ (2.5 cm) strip of fusible web around the outside edges of each building segment. The fusible web stabilizes the fabric to minimize fraying and helps hold the fabrics to the batting.

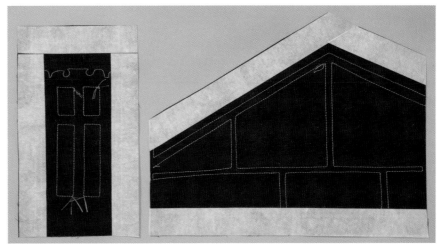

Press strip of fusible web around outside edges.

6. Trim from the front, leaving ⅛˝ (3 mm) margin of dark base fabric around each segment. Remember that some edges will have the under/overlap, and these are not trimmed.

Trim edges that will be visible.

7. After removing the backing paper from the fusible web strips, add the various building segments in order, checking the placement.

Put wall segment in place.

8. Press the segments in place and add extra pins if necessary.

9. Using a fine, matching dark thread, stitch around the dark edge of each segment, through the quilt sandwich, to hold it in place. For straight-line stitching, use a walking foot or dual feed foot; for curvy lines or lines that change direction often, use free-motion stitching.

Add roof segment.

TIP ⁓ If you are having trouble seeing through the tracing-paper pattern, trace the pattern on clear vinyl, which is easier to see through than tracing paper.

10. Finally add the foreground, stitching along the dark edge.

Add and stitch foreground.

TIP ⁓ For larger designs it may be helpful to stitch features such as windows and doors to the walls before appliquéing segments together on the sandwich.

Quilt and Finish

1. Stitch-in-the-ditch around the main features, and then add more texture with quilting lines.

2. Add a border, narrow binding, or finish with a faced edge (see Finishing, page 95).

BONUS **DOWNLOAD** ▶ You can make your own *Robe Custom House* while you learn the basic techniques. To download the *Robe Custom House* pattern, see How to Use This Book (page 6). Then print it out at home on 8½″ × 11″ (A4) paper and tile it together. Use the techniques from *Seaside Cottage* to put it together.

Robe Custom House

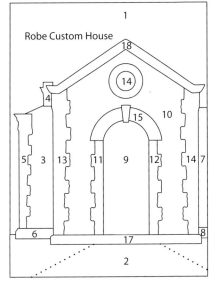

Robe Custom House by Gloria Loughman, 15½″ × 21½″ (40 cm × 54 cm)

SPECIAL FEATURES

Multiple Buildings

Rather than basing a design on just one building, this example features a group of colorful buildings overlooking the river in Girona in Spain. If you design a quilt that features a number of buildings, draw the pattern including the buildings and their features. Don't get bogged down in the details, simplifying where necessary.

Inspiration photo of Girona, Spain

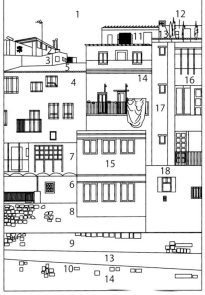

Simplified drawing of buildings on riverside at Girona

To make the project manageable when working with multiple buildings, trace the outline of each of the main buildings and work on them individually. Numbering the buildings in the order that they will be appliquéd to the sandwich will keep things in order. Some of these main walls will not need a dark base—later in the process, a strip of dark base fabric can be fused to the back of any edge that will be visible when the quilt is constructed. The *Italian Village* (page 105) uses this process. Each building is made separately then stitched together on the sandwich.

TIP It may be easier to manage if a smaller tracing is made of each building rather than having to check accurate placement with the original large sheet of tracing paper.

Napa Riverfront
by Michelle M. Moore,
24″ × 40″ (61 cm × 102 cm)

Multiple buildings with river foreground and vineyard hills and sky in background

Stone Walls

1. Using the freezer-paper pattern as a guide, prepare the base for the stone wall. Choose the color of the base to match the cement in the stone wall. This needs to contrast with the stones themselves, so audition fabric for the stones first and then choose a suitable base. This can be the dark base fabric used throughout the design or another fabric.

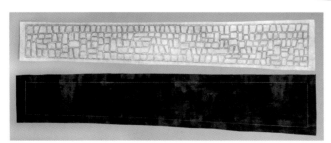

Prepare base and draw stone wall on fusible web.

2. Either trace or draw in the stones on the paper side of the fusible web. Remember the scale of the stones needs to be in proportion to the rest of the design. Press this fusible web to the back of the selected stone fabric.

Press fusible web to back of stone fabric.

3. Cut out each stone, remove the fusible backing paper, and place the stone in position on the base.

Another example of stones placed on base

4. After all the stones have been placed in position, stitch around each one using a matching or variegated thread. Use free-motion stitching, continuing the stitching from one stone to the next.

TIP ⌇ If any of the stitching stands out on the base fabric between the stones, color it in with a Sharpie so that it becomes invisible.

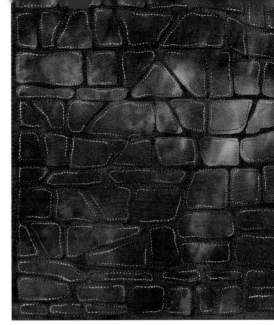

Detail of stone wall in *Merrill Hall, Asilomar* (page 63)

Detail of bricks in *Changing Rooms at the Geelong Outdoor Sea Baths* (page 8)

There are some buildings where only a section of the stonework is exposed. To make this look realistic, use a fabric for the stones that is similar or the same as the wall adjacent to it.

Photo by Neil Porter

Venetian Facade by Elaine Blundell, 24″ × 35″ (61 cm × 89 cm)

Effective combination of brick and stone

Lisa's Wee Hoose by Wendy Burrowes, 23″ × 34½″ (58 cm × 88 cm)

Beautiful stonework house

Windows

Windows usually have a frame or multiple frames around the glass. When constructing windows, it is customary to start with the glass, add the first frame, and finally the outside frame. Proceeding this way will add perspective to the window. At times, however, it is much easier to start with a rectangle for the outside frame, add a smaller rectangle for the next frame, and finally a small rectangle for the glass, building these layers up on a dark base. Either method will work; just remember that although the first technique will give more perspective, you will have to add the necessary under/overlaps so that you are overlapping and not leaving gaps.

For fabric selections that work well for glass, see Fabric for Glass (page 38).

Window built up from glass outward

A wonderful thing about windows is that they often have reflections—they can be a focal point or a more subtle feature for the viewer to enjoy on closer examination.

Subtle reflections in detail of *Old Bank Building, Kilmore* (page 30)

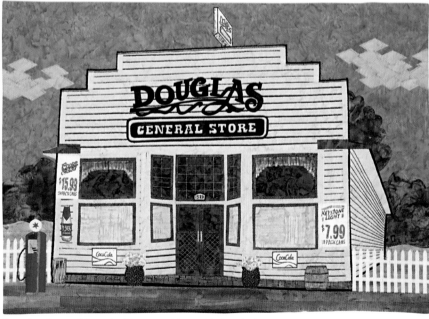

Douglas General Store by Margaret Meier, 30½˝ × 21½˝ (77 cm × 55 cm)

Various eye-catching reflections in the windows of *Changing Rooms at the Geelong Outdoor Sea Baths* (page 8)

Images of shops are a wonderful source for design. The windows can be full of intriguing shapes and the text provides further interest.

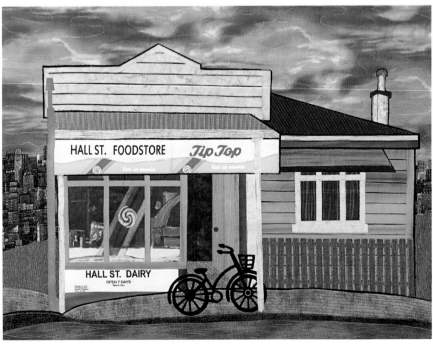

Hall St. Dairy by Liz McKenzie, 26″ × 20″ (66 cm × 51 cm)

Wrought Iron

Wrought iron gates or detailed trim around verandas and doors provide interesting detail to a facade. These effects can be achieved in fabric, stitching, or by adding appropriate lace. These details are usually applied toward the end of the construction.

Southall by Anna Rackham, 32½″ × 28½″ (83 cm × 72 cm)

42 Alpha Road by Sue Morgan, 14″ × 20″ (36 cm × 51 cm)

Detail of lace used on balcony

Detail of lace used on veranda post

backgrounds AND FOREGROUNDS

As part of the design process, you have the option of cropping an original image (see Cropping, page 18), filling the whole frame with the facade, or you can leave in some of the background or foreground. You have to decide how much of the setting is necessary and sufficient to create the mood you want. Backgrounds and foregrounds that are not interesting in real life will not be interesting in your piece. Be sure that the background and foreground do not overwhelm the facade, and that they support the facade appropriately.

Many techniques can be used to create the different pieces of background or foreground in a design. The setting can be realistic or implied—the choice is yours.

BACKGROUND—SKY

You need to think about a number of considerations when planning the sky. Taking into account the area of sky you have in the design, decide whether you would like it to be realistic or abstract. The color is also an important design decision.

Commercial Sky Fabric

Some beautiful commercial fabrics work well for sky. Use them wisely, where you want movement and interest in the background. Check to see that they don't overpower the building but just provide something special. Always position the darkest area at the top of the sky, getting lighter as it moves toward the horizon.

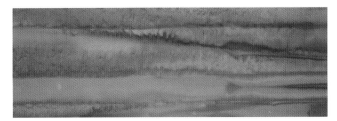

Commercial fabric provides movement in sky.

Remembrance of Home by Donna M. MacDonald, 34″ × 26½″ (86 cm × 67 cm)

Donna's quilt features batik fabric for sky.

Merrill Hall, Asilomar by Gloria Loughman, 32″ × 44″ (81 cm × 112 cm)

Painted Sky

If you are looking for a sky that is unique and gives perspective to the design, then unpack your fabric paints and have some fun—refer to my book *Radiant Landscapes* (from C&T Publishing) for painting techniques.

Hand-painted sky provides good contrast with color of building of *Robe Custom House* (page 57).

Collage Sky

Collage techniques allow you to simplify shapes and manipulate colors to achieve unique results. You also have the opportunity to move the shapes around until you are happy with the composition. Shapes that I have used in the sky in many of my quilts include diamonds and rectangular strips.

Strips

1. Press the freezer-paper sky pattern onto the chosen base fabric. You can choose whether this base fabric is visible in some places later in the process. Keeping this in mind, it is good to choose a fabric that blends with the fabric you have selected for the strips.

2. Cut out the base fabric with a generous 1″ (2.5 cm) seam allowance around the outside.

TIP After you remove the freezer paper, use a chalk pen to draw a series of horizontal lines 2″ (5 cm) apart on the sky base fabric. These lines will help you position the strips accurately.

3. Press a repositionable fusible web, such as Lite Steam-A-Seam 2, to the back of the fabrics you have selected for the strips. Using a rotary cutter, cut strips at varying widths, keeping in mind the area to be covered. Strips can be cut at widths from ⅜″ (1 cm) to 1½″ (3.8 cm). Vary the length of the strips, although this can be manipulated later in the process as you arrange them on the surface.

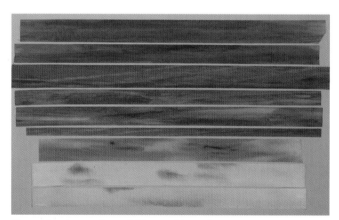

Cut strips in varying widths and lengths.

4. Arrange the strips in a pleasing sequence over the base. Strips can be overlapped or left separate, and you have a choice as to whether to cover the whole sky or leave areas of the base fabric showing through. Darker strips should be placed at the top and lighter ones toward the horizon line.

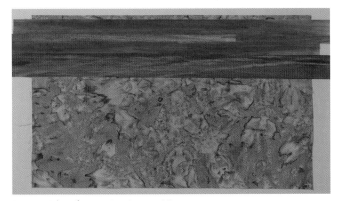

Base with a few strips in position

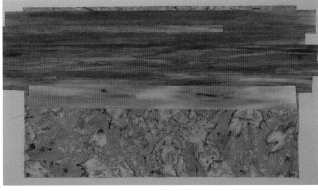

More strips added

Base with strips in position, ready to be trimmed at sides and pressed

Collage sky in *Merrill Hall, Asilomar* (page 63)

Portland Bungalow by Donna Moog, 34″ × 24″ (86 cm × 61 cm)

Collage background

Diamonds

1. To prepare the fabric base, follow the instructions as for Strips (page 64).

2. Draw chalk lines at a 60° angle to the side of the base every 2″ (5 cm).

3. Press a repositionable fusible web, such as Lite Steam-A-Seam 2, to the back of the fabrics you have selected for the diamonds. Using a rotary cutter, cut strips 1½″ (3.8 cm) wide. Line up the 60° line on a ruler along the top edge of a strip and cut across the end.

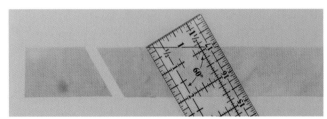

Continue to cut lines parallel to first cut at 1½″ (3.8 cm) intervals.

4. Arrange the diamonds on the base fabric. You can place them at regular intervals with a consistent gap in between or scatter them across the surface, overlapping and leaving areas of the base showing through. Follow the chalk lines to keep the diamonds on the same angle.

Overlap diamonds on background using guide lines.

5. Stitch the diamonds in place as part of the quilting process. An option for quilting is to stitch parallel lines, endeavoring to stitch down as many raw edges as possible.

TIP For more information on tiling techniques, refer to *Radiant Landscapes* by Gloria Loughman (from C&T Publishing).

Photo by C&T Publishing

Christchurch Cathedral by Linda Wagner, 26″ × 39″ (66 cm × 99 cm)

Squares placed on point make stunning background.

Butterfly House by Gloria Loughman, 44″ × 60″ (112 cm × 152 cm)

Overlapping diamonds are featured in sky, water, and foliage

One Piece of Fabric Sky

When a building contains a lot of detail, then a simple sky might be the perfect contrast to highlight the colors of the building and to keep the facade the center of interest.

BACKGROUND—FOREST

A background full of trees can be created using a variety of techniques. These include painting trees on fabric, collage with vertical rectangles, and commercial fabrics printed with forest designs.

Avery Treehouse by Diane E. Mitchell, 33½″ × 22″ (85 cm × 56 cm)

Commercial tree fabric is used very effectively behind building.

Still Watching in Bodega Bay by Jan Nilsen, 38″ × 57″ (97 cm × 145 cm)

Single fabric for sky provides wonderful contrast to building

Boathouses by Marnie Mascioli, 32″ × 25″ (81 cm × 64 cm)

Hand-painted sky with appliquéd forest and stitching provide wonderful backdrop.

Abstract Forest

For a more stylized forest, see the technique outlined in *Campervan* (page 115).

This technique, which has a more abstract feel, uses a variety of beautiful, textured fabrics.

FOREGROUND

The foreground of a design could be a simple body of water, a piece of lawn, or perhaps a paved footpath. The strip collage technique (page 64), works very well for water and even pieces of garden or bush. Keeping the shapes simple and arranging them to give a feeling of the setting will create interest but not take away from the facade.

Detail of *Campervan* (page 115)

Water

Water can be made from a single piece of fabric, but using strips of various fabrics adds detail and interest (see *Italian Village*, page 105).

Detail of water in *Italian Village* (page 105)

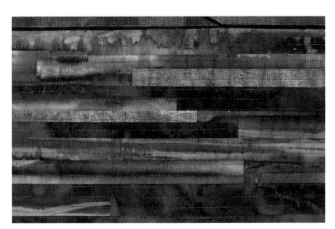

Detail of water in *Sydney Opera House, Vivid Festival* (page 22)

Paved Footpath

A simple paved section in the foreground of a design adds perspective and a quiet area of interest. Many varieties of paving can be replicated. A simple and manageable technique is to use a dark solid background and place cut-out paving stones on a dark base, leaving a small gap between them.

Paved foreground of *Geelong Fire Station* (page 76)

Yellow Cottage by Suzanne Gaensbauer, 24″ × 26″ (61 cm × 66 cm)

Paved sidewalk grounds facade

DOORWAYS

Doors have an intriguing and beguiling story to tell us. Doorways give us many possibilities. Architects have created some amazing doorways in a wide variety of shapes and materials. Artists have used doorways as a source of inspiration for many beautiful paintings. Photographers especially love doorways, and books have been published showcasing a myriad of incredible doorways from around the world.

Some doorways are elaborate and others are commonplace. They are created from many different materials and showcase a range of stunning colors and textures. Some of the more interesting doors are in less than perfect condition. They show their age as the materials weather, the paint fades and peels, and the metal rusts. Some doors are covered with graffiti and provide a canvas for street artists.

Doors provide a means from which we can move from one place to another. Open, they provide an invitation, a temptation, a mystery to be explored. Closed, a door can be a challenge, provide separation, or inspire a desire to find out what is on the other side.

Doorways from our travels

DESIGN

When considering the placement of a doorway, it is likely that the door will be placed central to the design. There are, of course, times when it will be placed off center, especially when you want to include other design elements such as a window.

Off-center doorway, balanced with window in Porto, Portugal

We found this wonderful old doorway when we were exploring in Peratallada, in Spain. The window is boarded up, the wood is weathered and rough and the metal doors are beginning to rust. A lot of character, so a perfect subject to create in fabric.

Spanish doorway central to design

Spanish Doorway by Gloria Loughman, 12″ × 17″, (30 cm × 43 cm)

BONUS ▶ DOWNLOAD You can make your own *Spanish Doorway* while you learn the basic techniques. To download the *Spanish Doorway* pattern, see How to Use This Book (page 6). Then print it out at home on 8½″ × 11″ (A4) paper and tile it together.

Preparation

For this example, I cropped the photo and used Sketch Guru to turn the photo in to a line drawing (see Using Apps, page 49).

1. Trace the main outline of the pattern onto good quality tracing paper. Go over key lines with a fine-point Sharpie so the image is clearly visible on the back of the tracing paper.

2. Trace the main segments onto the dull side of freezer paper. Number the pieces according to the order they will be placed on the batting

Pencil drawing using Sketch Guru

Trace design on tracing paper.

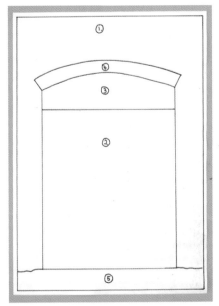

Trace main segments on freezer paper.

CONSTRUCTION

Refer to Construction (page 50).

Prepare the Base Pieces

1. Cut out the freezer-paper pieces and position them, shiny side down on the right side of the dark base fabric. After these have been pressed in place with a hot iron, cut around each one with at least a ½˝ (1.3 cm) seam allowance.

Freezer paper pressed to right side of dark fabric

2. With a good quality chalk pen, draw a fine line around each freezer-paper shape, ⅛˝ (3 mm) out from the freezer paper edge.

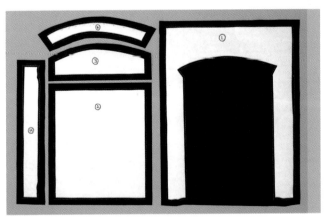

Bases ready to go

Add Fabric

1. Audition fabrics for the main building surfaces. Trace each piece from the back of the tracing paper onto repositionable paper-backed fusible web, such as such as Lite Steam-A-Seam 2. Add a ¼˝ (6 mm) under/overlap on any edge that will be later tucked under or go into the border. Cut out the shape from the fusible web leaving a small margin around the edge. Press the fusible web to the back of the selected fabric. Cut out the pieces on the line including the under/overlap where necessary.

2. Peel off the backing paper from the fusible web and position the pieces on the dark background fabric inside the chalk line, leaving ⅛˝ (3 mm) margin around the edge. Press the pieces in place. The pieces that have the extra under/overlap will cover the chalk guide line.

Cut out door and surround segments.

Position door segments on background fabric.

3. For brick, stone, paving, or timber, trace the outline of the shapes onto the fusible web before applying it to the back of the selected fabric (see Stone Walls, page 58). Cut out each piece trimming where necessary to form a small gap. Position them on the base fabric.

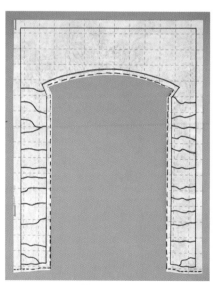

Trace stone wall onto fusible web.

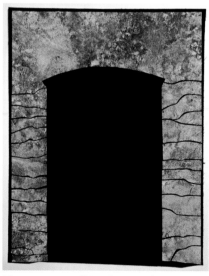

Place stone wall in place on base.

Prepare and place timber sections on base.

Prepare window segments

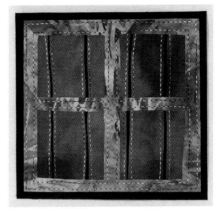

Put together window.

Add Stitching

After all the building surfaces are completed, stitch around the edge of each piece, using a straight stitch and matching colored thread. The edges that will be covered by the next piece or go in to the border of the quilt do not need to be stitched.

Put It Together

1. Press a 1˝ (2.5 cm) strip of fusible web, to any edge that will be visible. The fusible web will help stabilize the edge when it is trimmed back.

Press strip of fusible web to back of edge before trimming.

2. Trim the edge that is fused to ⅛˝ (3 mm).

Trim visible edges to ⅛˝ (3 mm).

3. Make up a quilt sandwich with the backing fabric and batting, allowing for the anticipated finishing (see Make the Quilt Sandwich, page 54).

TIP Remember to remove the pins from the quilt sandwich as you add the fabric on top.

4. Position the tracing-paper pattern on the batting leaving the appropriate margin. Mark the corners of the pattern on the batting to make it easy to replace the pattern on top of the pieces to check accurate placement.

5. Using the pattern as a guide, place segment 1 in position. For some designs, this piece will not have a dark base as all edges will be covered by subsequent pieces or they will go in to the border of the quilt. Pin the segments in place with straight pins.

6. Add segment 2, overlapping the edges of segment 1 where appropriate. Stitch along dark edge in a matching colored fine thread, stitching through the quilt sandwich.

Place segment 2 in position.

7. Add subsequent segments in order, stitching along the dark edges.

Quilt and Finish

1. When all the segments are stitched in position, add quilting to the various surfaces.

2. Finish the quilt with a border, binding, or faced edge (see Finishing, page 95).

SPECIAL DOORWAYS

Doors can be constructed from many different materials. These quilts feature a range of materials for the door and doorway plus some wonderful decorative elements.

Old Geelong Fire Station by Gloria Loughman, 12½″ × 18″ (32 cm × 46 cm)

Old wooden boards feature prominently in doorway.

Photo by Ashleigh Ward

Portal by Lynne Rowe, 16½″ × 24″ (42 cm × 61 cm)

Door features glass panels and stonework.

Time Reveals by Suzann Moss, 16½″ × 19″ (42 cm × 48 cm)

Fabulous textured surface and striking metal work

Old Library Door by Ngaire Fleming, 16″ × 23½″ (41 cm × 60 cm)

Stunning old timber door and regal surrounds

Photo by Andrew Lincoln

#41 by JoAnne Lincoln, 24″ × 36″ (61 cm × 91 cm)

Wrought iron adorns colorful doorway.

Church Manse—Madeline island, WI, USA, by Gloria Loughman, 12½˝ × 18½˝ (32 cm × 47 cm)

Angled boards and oval window are features of doorway.

other FACADES

The technique that you have been using to make the building designs can also be used to create other subjects. Virtually anything that has a surface can be created in fabric using this outline technique.

Lighthouses, trucks, caravans, old cars, ships, and trains are wonderful sources of inspiration. Rather than starting with a building, consider some of the other images you have always wanted to create in fabric.

Tug on colorful waterway in Brisbane

Abandoned locomotive in Port Augusta, South Australia

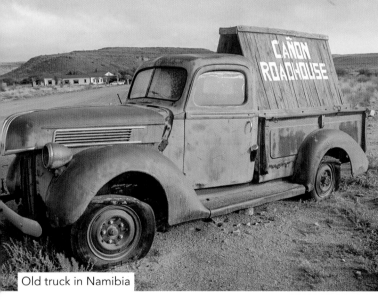

Old truck in Namibia

Old tug, full of character in Queensland, Australia

CARGO SHIP DESIGN

One wet, cloudy day, we took a ferry trip around the Port of Seattle. The different colored containers on the ship, provided a wonderful contrast both in color and shape and added to the frenetic pace involved in unloading and loading in a busy port. The text on the ship and the port provided further focal points of interest. To balance these details, a strong colored sky and a simplification of the port structure helped to bring the design together.

Original image in Port of Seattle

Cargo Ship by Gloria Loughman, 31″ × 25″ (79 cm × 64 cm)

Preparation

BONUS DOWNLOAD You can make your own *Cargo Ship* while you learn the basic techniques. To download the *Cargo Ship* pattern, see How to Use This Book (page 6). Then print it out at home on 8½″ × 11″ (A4) paper and tile it together.

Refer to Creating the Pattern (page 42) and Construction (page 50).

I simplified the original photo and changed some of the lines of the ship slightly so that the ship is now viewed from directly behind, and some of the horizontal lines on the dock have been redrawn using a vanishing point (see Using Perspective, page 43).

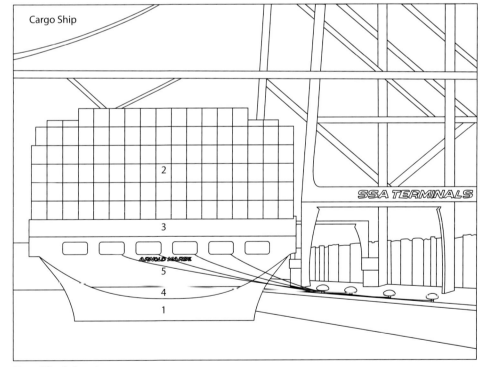

Simplified drawing

TIP With so many different pieces to create, it's best to construct the main elements separately and then appliqué them together on the quilt sandwich.

CONSTRUCTION

Refer to Construction (page 50).

Make the Ship

Prepare the Base Pieces

1. Trace the ship onto the dull side of freezer paper. Number the sections in the order that they will be appliquéd later in the process.

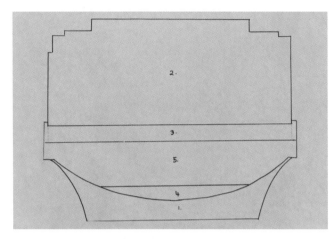

Original drawing on freezer-paper pattern

The ship has been broken down in to 5 main pieces with an extension made on piece 2 to go under piece 3.

Draw extension on freezer-paper pattern 2.

2. Cut out the freezer-paper patterns and press them to the right side of the dark base fabric. Cut them out with a generous ½″ (1.3 cm) seam allowance.

3. Using a fine chalk marker, draw a line around the edge of each shape, ⅛″ (3 mm) out from the edge of the freezer paper.

Draw around each shape.

4. Remove the freezer paper

Add Fabric

1. After selecting fabrics for surfaces 1, 3, 4, and 5, trace these shapes from the back of the tracing-paper pattern onto repositionable paper-backed fusible web. Add an under/overlap margin on the edges that will tuck under the next segment. On shapes 3 and 5, also trace the windows.

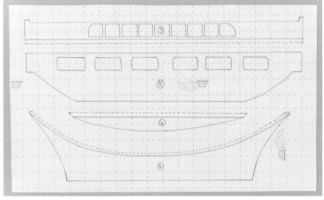

Add under/overlap margins.

2. Cut out the fusible web shapes with a small margin around the outside. Press the fusible web shape to the back of the selected fabrics. Cut them out on the line, including the added margins where necessary. Carefully cut out the windows on pieces 3 and 5.

Cut out windows.

TIP A small rotary cutter or knife can be very handy for accurately cutting out windows and other small pieces.

3. Press each of these fabrics to its corresponding base, overlapping the chalk line where there is an added margin.

Press fabric to base.

4. In matching thread and using a straight stitch, stitch around the edge of the fabric and around the windows.

Make the Containers

1. Measure the size of one container on the pattern. Take off ⅛″ (3 mm) from the width and height so the containers can be loaded with a narrow gap between.

2. Select the fabrics for the containers and apply fusible web to the back. Cut out the rectangles for the containers using a rotary cutter.

3. Peel off the backing paper and position each container on base 2, leaving a gap of approximately ⅛″ (3 mm) between each container. Make the colors random but asymmetrically balanced. The brighter colors will stand out, so scatter these across the load.

Place containers on base fabric.

4. Stitch the containers in place. A variegated thread works well where the stitching is across many different colors.

Make the Lettering

1. Trace the terminal letters from the reverse side of the tracing-paper pattern to onto fusible web. Cut them out with a margin and press to the back of the selected fabric. Cut out each letter individually and place it in position using the pattern as a guide. Using a fine thread and needle, stitch the letters in place.

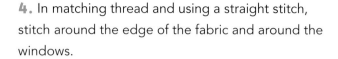

Place cut-out letters on terminal.

2. The letters on the ship are much smaller and made using the programmed stitches on the sewing machine. Coloring in the letters with a permanent fabric pen makes them stand out.

Stitch and fill in letters on ship.

Make the Ship Trim

1. Press fusible web to the back of each section.

2. Cut out the windows leaving a narrow edge of black.

3. Cut around the edges of the shapes that will be visible, leaving a ⅛″ (3 mm) edge of dark fabric. Do not trim the edges with the seam allowances.

Trim edges that will be visible.

Make the Background and Foreground

After the parts of the ship have been made, it is time to work on the background. The background is made up of the terminal, the sea, and the sky.

Make the Terminal

1. Trace segments A, B, C, and D onto the dull side of freezer paper.

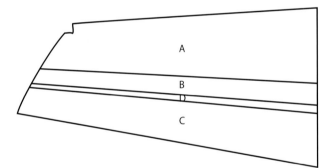

Terminal segments A, B, C, and D.

2. Cut out shapes A, B, and D and press them onto the dark base fabric. Cut out these shapes with a generous ½″ (1.3 cm) seam allowance. Draw a line around the freezer paper ⅛″ (3 mm) out from the edge. Remove the freezer paper.

3. Choose fabrics for these pieces.

4. Trace the outline of shapes A, B, and D from the back of the pattern onto fusible web. Add an under/overlap margin on the bottom edge of shapes A and B and to all side edges.

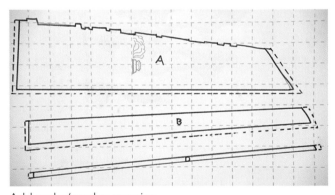

Add under/overlap margins.

5. Cut out the fusible web with a small margin around the outside of the shape and press to the back of the selected fabrics. Cut out on the line including seam allowances where they have been added.

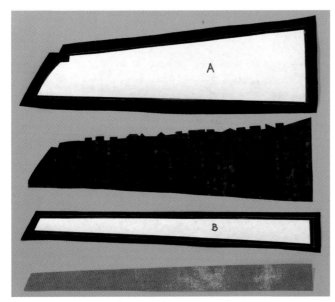

Prepare bases A and B and shapes A and B.

Fuse shapes A and B to bases, and fuse D to its corresponding base.

Add stitched detail to shape A.

Make the Area Under the Terminal

Piece C is a body of water under the terminal and includes the pylons holding up the wharf; it does not need a dark base.

1. Choose a fabric for the water, remembering there is not much light here so the fabric should be darker than the rest of the water.

2. Press the freezer-paper shape C to the right side of this dark water fabric and cut it out with a ½″ (1.3 cm) margin around the outside.

3. Draw a chalk line ⅛″ (3 mm) out from the freezer paper edge before removing the freezer paper.

4. Choose the fabric for the pylons and apply fusible web to the back. Cut out the pylons, remembering they will be getting shorter in length and width as they move toward the distance. The space between the pylons will also get smaller. It may be helpful to trace out this section onto its own sheet of tracing paper to get the perspective accurate.

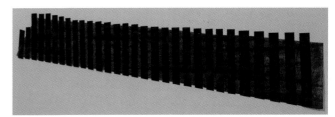

Add pylons to water fabric.

5. Trim the overlapping edges of the pylons. Stitch the edges of the pylons with a straight stitch.

Make the Sky

1. Trace the sky outline onto the dull side of freezer paper and cut it out on the line.

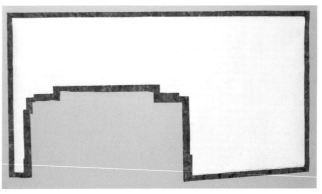

Cut out sky, adding ½″ margin

2. Choose the fabric for the sky and press the freezer-paper pattern to the right side of this fabric. (For help choosing sky fabric, see Fabrics for Sky, page 38, and Backgrounds and Foregrounds—Sky, page 63.)

3. Cut out the sky adding a ½″ (1.3 cm) margin around the outside of the freezer-paper pattern.

Make the Sea

The sea can be one fabric or a number of different fabric strips overlapping on a base. The sea for this sample was made using strips (see Water, page 69). If you are using one fabric, press the freezer-paper pattern to the sea fabric and cut out with a generous seam allowance of ½″ (1.3 cm) around the outside. If you have decided to add strips, then proceed the same way, using this fabric as the base.

Make the Loading Equipment

1. Trace all the elements of the loading equipment from the back of the freezer-paper pattern onto fusible web.

2. Cut out each element with a small margin, then press these shapes to the back of the selected fabrics. Some elements will need an under/overlap margin added when they sit under the edge of another piece of equipment. Cut out the shapes on the line adding the margins where necessary.

3. Remove the backing paper from the fusible web and press these shapes onto dark base fabric.

Cut out shapes with narrow edge of dark fabric around outside.

Press shapes to dark base fabric.

4. Apply fusible web to the back of the dark base and then cut out the shapes with a small, narrow edge of dark fabric around each shape

5. Apply fusible web to the back of the fabric to be used for the straight strips of the loading equipment. Cut out the strips with a rotary cutter at the appropriate width. Fuse the strips to a piece of dark base fabric.

Fuse strips to base fabric.

6. Apply fusible web to the back of the base fabric and cut out the strips with a narrow dark edge.

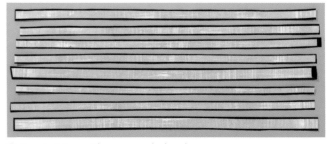

Cut out strips with narrow dark edges.

PUT IT TOGETHER

1. Make the quilt sandwich. Cut the batting and backing fabric, allowing a 2″ (5 cm) margin around the outside of the pattern. (Refer to Make the Quilt Sandwich, page 54.)

2. Position the tracing-paper pattern on the batting and mark in the corners.

3. Place the sky fabric in place on the batting, checking placement with the tracing-paper pattern.

TIP ∼ Remember to remove the pins from the quilt sandwich as you add the fabric on top.

4. Place the sea in position, checking the placement with the tracing-paper pattern overlay.

Sky and sea in position

5. It is a good idea to quilt the sky and sea now while there is a clear run across the surface. Variegated threads are a good choice for the water. It is important to keep the quilting lines mainly horizontal. Try to capture the top edge of the different strips when stitching.

6. Add the other background pieces in order: first background A and then backgrounds C and B. The lower edge of A is overlapped by B. C overlaps the water at the bottom edge and will eventually be under shape D at the top edge. Shape D will overlap the bottom edge of B and the top edge of C.

Add background A and C.

Add background B.

7. Add the dock equipment. Using the pattern as a guide, place the appropriate strips in position and press them down. Stitch down along the narrow dark edge in a fine, dark thread.

Working from back to front, fuse strips in place.

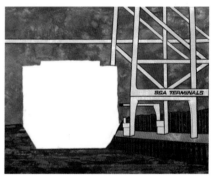

Add remaining structure.

8. Add the container ship. Checking for accurate placement, fuse the various sections in position overlapping where necessary. As each section is added, stitch around the dark narrow edge to hold it in position.

Add narrow strip D.

Add container ship pieces in order.

9. Add the small posts on the dock, and then stitch the ropes from the ships to these points. Use a triple stitch so that the ropes are visible.

Add small posts and triple stitch ropes.

Quilt

As the water and sky are already quilted, the only other areas left to quilt are the dock and the ship. Quilt between containers and inside the window frames. Add additional quilting lines to the dock area if desired.

Finish

A lot of options are available for finishing the edges of a quilt. As the color scheme for this quilt is vibrant and strong, I decided to finish the edges with a facing (see Finishing, page 95).

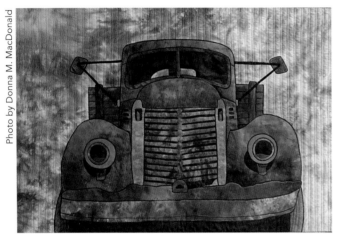

Photo by Donna M. MacDonald

Rusty by Donna M. MacDonald, 40½″ × 28″ (103 cm × 71 cm)

Old Tender on Norfolk Island by Gloria Loughman, 16½″ × 24½″ (42 cm × 62 cm)

SKYSCRAPERS

When visiting the wonderfully vibrant city of New York, I am in danger of wiping out fellow pedestrians as I wander the streets, continually looking up. Spectacular, innovative, ingenious, controversial are all adjectives that describe many of the super-tall buildings that have been constructed over the past one hundred years or so.

These towering giants, many of which seem to defy gravity, inspire awe and excitement.

Around the world many spectacular buildings draw visitors. They can also provide wonderful inspiration for artists.

Most modern skyscrapers are characterized by large surface areas of windows interspersed with steel, frames, and walls. The shapes, color, and combinations of these components provide the opportunity for wonderful repetitive patterns that can be a starting place for innovative quilt designs. Although the building may be uniform or even sometimes "bland" in color, imagine using a palette of fabrics to create a stunning and unique image.

DESIGN

Tall buildings provide a wonderful collection of patterns that can be created in fabric. The inspiration for this quilt was an office block in the business district of Melbourne. Not a very exciting building as such, but the repetition of the pattern of the windows, gave me the opportunity to take the design and then fill it in with color and texture.

The building was made up of a series of blocks each one made up of two sheets of glass, a vertical upright, a horizontal bar, and a frame.

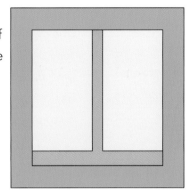

Simplified block

This design is a bit different from the other facades in this book in that it is made using a repeated block design. For this example, I decided that the blocks would measure 6½″ × 6½″ (16.5 cm × 16.5 cm) and would be appliquéd together to form a 3 × 5 grid.

Skyscraper by Gloria Loughman, 24″ × 37½″ (61 cm × 95 cm)

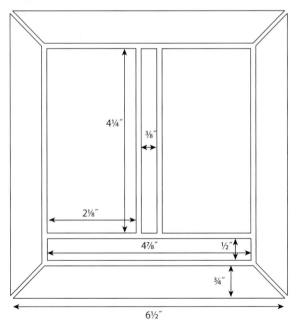

Measured block; gaps measure ⅛″ (3 mm).

BLOCK CONSTRUCTION

Prepare the Bases

Each block is constructed on a dark base with the elements fused in place with a narrow gap in between. The size of the base needs to be ½″ (1.3 cm) bigger around the outside edges of the block.

1. Cut the desired number of 7½″ × 7½″ (19 cm × 19 cm) squares of dark fabric. In this example there are 15 blocks.

2. Draw a fine chalk line ½″ (1.3 cm) in from each side, so there is a 6½″ × 6½″ (16.5 cm × 16.5 cm) drawn square centered on the base fabric. Use a 6½″ × 6½″ (16.5 cm × 16.5 cm) square ruler if you have one.

Draw chalk line.

Make the Outside Window Frames

1. Choose a fabric for the outside frame that works well and provides some contrast with the glass fabric.

2. Press paper-backed fusible web to the back of this frame fabric.

3. Cut the prepared fabric so you have a total of 60 strips ¾″ × 6½″ (1.9 cm × 16.5 cm).

4. Using the 45° line on the ruler, cut off the corners.

Cut off corners at 45°.

5. Position these strips with the outside edges on the chalk line. There will be a small gap in each corner.

Place strips with small gaps in corners to form window frame.

Make the Glass Windows

1. As the glass panes are the largest elements, choose a fabric that is eye-catching and interesting. Consider some of the spectacular digitally printed commercial fabrics or something you have created yourself.

2. Press paper-backed fusible web on the back of this fabric and cut 2 rectangles 2⅛″ by 4¼″ (5.4 cm × 10.8 cm) for each block for a total of 30.

3. Position these shapes inside the frame leaving a narrow gap in each corner.

Place glass panes, leaving narrow gap.

Make the Vertical and Horizontal Beams

1. Choose a fabric that contrasts but works well with the frame and glass fabric. Press the fusible web to the back of the fabric, and cut 15 strips ⅜″ × 4¼″ (1 cm × 10.8 cm) and 15 strips ½″ × 4⅞″ (1.3 cm × 12.4 cm).

2. Place the narrower strip vertically between the two glass panes, leaving a narrow gap on each side.

3. Place the wider strip horizontally, leaving the narrow gaps.

Place vertical and horizontal beams.

Stitch

Stitch around each shape with a matching or a variegated thread that mirrors the colors in the fabrics. Use a straight stitch and stitch ⅛″ (3 mm) in from the edge. All the raw edges need to be stitched.

PUT IT TOGETHER

After all the blocks have been constructed and stitched, it is time to appliqué the blocks together.

Prepare the Quilt Sandwich

1. Cut the batting and backing fabric 28″ × 42″ (71 cm × 107 cm) and sandwich them together (see Make the Quilt Sandwich, page 54). This measurement allows for a narrow border or it may be trimmed if a facing or narrow binding will be applied (see Finishing, page 95).

2. Draw horizontal and vertical lines on the batting to help with accurate placement of the blocks.

Join the Blocks

Arrange the blocks in the grid striving for a pleasing asymmetrical balance. Number the blocks by writing on masking tape and attaching to front.

Row 1

1. Starting on the bottom row, press a 1″ (2.5 cm) strip of fusible web to the left hand side edge of blocks 2 and 3 on the back of the fabric. Trim the edge so that only ¼″ (6 mm) of the base fabric shows.

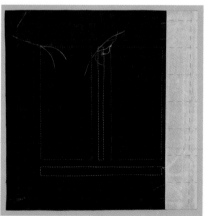
Apply fusible web to back of left hand side and trim.

13	14	15
10	11	12
7	8	9
4	5	6
1	2	3

Numbering plan

TIP ⁓ Trim only after you have applied the fusible web to the back as this stabilizes the raw edge to prevent fraying.

2. Place block 1 in position on the sandwich and pin. Overlay the left edge of block 2 over the right edge of block 1, and press the edges with the fusible web.

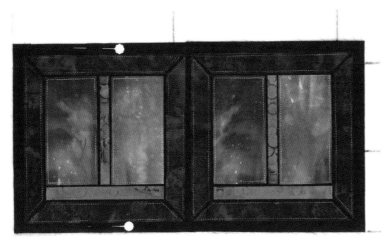

Overlap block 2 on block 1.

3. Repeat this process with block 3, overlapping the left edge of block 2.

TIP ∼ Remember to remove the pins from the quilt sandwich as you add the fabric on top.

4. Using a walking foot, stitch along both sides of the overlapped edges with a straight stitch, using a dark thread to hold the edges in place.

TIP ∼ It is preferable to stitch with a walking foot to keep the layers of the quilt sandwich from shifting as you stitch.

Row 2

1. Press a 1″ (2.5 cm) strip of fusible web to the bottom edge of block 4 and trim so that only ¼″ (6 mm) of the base fabric shows on this edge.

2. Matching up vertical lines, place block 4 in position, with the trimmed edge overlapping the top edge of block 1. Press.

3. Press a 1″ (2.5 cm) strip of fusible web to the bottom edge and the left side edge of blocks 5 and 6. Trim as in Step 1.

4. Place blocks 5 and 6 in position overlapping the top edges of blocks 2 and 3 and the right hand side edges of blocks 4 and 5. Check that the lines match up.

5. Stitch along the overlapping vertical edges and the lower edge of row 2 in a dark matching thread, stitching right through the sandwich. Stitch both sides of the ¼″ (6 mm) overlap.

Rows 3, 4, and 5

Repeat Row 2, Steps 1–5, for rows 3, 4, and 5.

All blocks in place on batting

Quilt

Start by quilting the vertical lines between the blocks and then quilt-in-the-ditch around the various elements. You can use a decorative stitch or stay with a straight stitch. You can add more quilting at this stage or decide that the quilt is finished and just needs a border, binding, or faced edge.

Add Borders

You have many options for borders. You could incorporate parts of the pattern in the border or decide on a strong simple frame to add cohesion. A narrow border in the same black fabric was added to the sample shown. The border strips were cut at 2½˝ (6.4 cm) and then added to the sides and then top and bottom edges.

With right sides together, stitch border strip to edge.

These borders were then pressed out flat and the sandwich was trimmed so that it was symmetrical. A faced edge (see Finishing, page 95) was then applied.

Alternative Fabric Choice

Although the initial block for this design is quite simple, the choice of fabric and its placement can provide a myriad of designs and effects. This second sample block was made using the same block design with commercial fabrics: a mottled gray around the outside, the commercial printed fabric for the panes, and a textured red and yellow to alternate in the blocks as the framework for the windows. This time the edge was finished with a facing and no extra borders were added. The final effect is very different to the first sample.

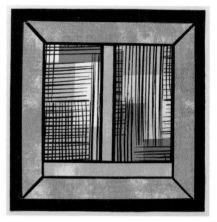

Same block design using commercial fabrics

Complete quilt with very different effect

ALTERNATIVE BLOCKS

The blocks used for the Skyscraper design were based on a square grid. Many other wonderful patterns have been used by architects. It is possible to break down many of these designs into repeating shapes. Using the overlapping method of construction, these blocks can be easily appliquéd together.

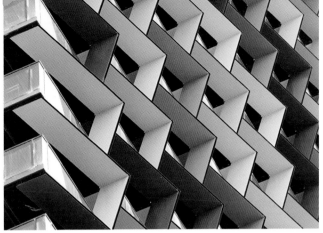

Original building photo

Looking at a cropped black and white image, an irregular, repeating outline becomes evident.

This block was drawn out to scale and a number of different size blocks were considered.

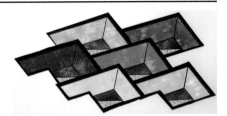

Starting to put design together

Cropped image using Sketch Guru (page 49)

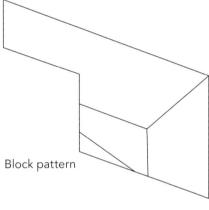

Block pattern

The various parts of the block were traced separately from the back of the pattern onto fusible web. These drawn shapes were then cut out with a small margin around the outside. After auditioning a range of fabrics, a mixed collection of patterned and textured fabrics was selected.

Base shape with freezer paper

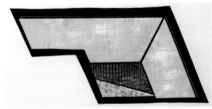

Single block in fabric

More blocks added

OTHER DESIGNS

Buildings offer a wonderful source of inspiration and patterns that you can replicate and repeat to make stunning and appealing designs. Using this technique of breaking down the design in to a simple block, you can make our own architectural quilt, using some of the amazing fabrics available today. This group of blocks features a fabric that is printed with skyscrapers, giving the effect of buildings being reflected in the glass.

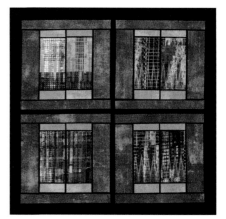

Skyscraper fabric used in windows

Walk around the city and look up at the friendly giants that tower over you. Look for patterns that are appealing and can be replicated in fabric. They are a never-ending source of inspiration once you start coloring them with your own palette of exciting colors and textures.

One Maritime Plaza, San Francisco

Maritime Plaza by Gloria Loughman, 21½″ × 36″ (55 cm × 91 cm)

FINISHING

You have many options for finishing the outside edge of the quilt. These options include mounting the quilt in a solid frame, adding borders, using a narrow binding, and finishing with a faced edge.

Borders and binding create a sense of completion and add definition to the outer edge. If a section of the design is light in color, it may need a binding and/or border so that it doesn't just disappear on the wall.

Some of the smaller quilts, such as the doorways, lend themselves to being mounted and framed. Alternatively, I finish many of my smaller pieces with a narrow binding as I feel they need that delineation. (For other finishing techniques, refer to my book *Radiant Landscapes*, from C&T Publishing.)

When you cut batting and backing for the quilt sandwich, be sure to allow for the anticipated finishing; for example, adding extra around the edges for borders or allowing extra fabric to wrap around a frame.

Photo by Neil Porter

Spires of St Basils by Jane Hopkins, 34″ × 31″ (86 cm × 79 cm)

Narrow border gives sense of completion.

Architecture in a Stark Landscape by Lesley Pearce, 15½″ × 21½″ (39 cm × 55 cm)

Strong formal dark border complements modern building.

FACED EDGES

This chapter focuses on using a faced edge, which has a contemporary feel and works well with the style of quilts featured in this book.

Comobella Hall by Ann Traynor, 24″ × 14½″ (61 cm × 37 cm)

Faced edge is excellent choice.

1. Square up the quilt sandwich using a large cutting mat and ruler to ensure accuracy. It is very important to have straight edges and square corners at this stage.

2. Measure through the vertical center of the quilt. For the side facings, cut 2 strips, 4½″ (11.4 cm) wide by the vertical center length. With the wrong sides together, press each strip in half lengthwise. I usually try to use the same fabric as the backing fabric on my quilt. The width of this strip is just a guide and can be adjusted depending on the size of the quilt.

3. Place the folded strip on the front of the quilt, along a side edge. Carefully align the raw edges. Using a walking foot, sew the facing to the quilt with an accurate ¼″ (6 mm) seam.

4. Repeat this process on the opposite side of the quilt.

Stitch facing to side edge on front of quilt.

5. Press this facing flat, away from the quilt. Stitch a row of under stitching ⅛″ (3 mm) away from the seamline on the facing.

On right side, press facing flat and then understitch.

6. Fold and press the facing around to the back of the quilt. Pin, and then slipstitch the facing to the back of the quilt. Repeat on the other side.

Press facing to back for hand stitching.

7. Measure through the horizontal center line and cut 2 strips, 4½″ (11 cm) by this length, plus 1″ (2.5 cm). Press this strip in half lengthwise with the wrong sides together.

8. Position the folded strips along the top and bottom edges of the quilt, making sure the facing extends past each end by ½″ (1.3 cm). Pin. Using a walking foot, sew the top and bottom strips to the front of the quilt.

9. Repeat Step 5 for the top and bottom facings.

10. Folding in the extra ½″ (1.3 cm) at each end, fold and press the entire facing to the back of the quilt, ready to be stitched in place. Pin. Check that the corners are nice and square, then slipstitch in place.

11. Add a hanging sleeve and label with the relevant information about your work of art.

Facing extends past top edge by ½″ (1.3 cm).

Sydney Harbor and Opera House by Donna Jacobs, 36″ × 24¾″ (91 cm × 63 cm)

Faced edge works well with strong sky color.

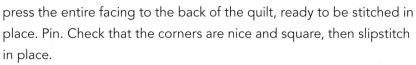

Photo by C&T Publishing

OLD DOORWAY   **FINISHED QUILT:** 11½″ × 17″ (29 cm × 43 cm)

This project features a classical old doorway with a plaster archway and old textured doors. For more inspiration, see Doorways (page 71).

Fabric Requirements

Base: ½ yard (0.5 m) dark batik or similar

Wall: 1 fat quarter (46 cm × 56 cm)

Door inside panels: 1 fat eighth (23 cm × 56 cm)

Door framework: 1 fat eighth (23 cm × 56 cm)

Side panels: 8″ × 8″ (20 cm × 20 cm)

Foreground: 1 fat eighth (23 cm × 56 cm)

Arch: 12″ × 18″ (30 cm × 46 cm)

Facing or binding: ¼ yard (25 cm)

Backing: 1 fat quarter (46 cm × 56 cm)

OTHER SUPPLIES

Freezer paper: ½ yard (0.5 m), 18″ (46 cm) wide

Tracing paper: 1 sheet 13″ × 18″ (33 cm × 46 cm) good quality 29 lb. (110 gsm)

Fusible web: 1 yard (1 m), 24″-wide repositionable paper-backed (Lite Steam-A-Seam 2 or similar)

Batting: 16″ × 21″ (41 cm × 53 cm)

Threads: To blend with selected fabrics

Colorful doorway in Porto Portugal

Old doorway in Spain

Rustic doorway in Spain

PREPARATION

Before starting this project, read through Doorways (page 71).

1. Photocopy the *Old Doorway* pattern (page 104). Or download the pattern (see instructions in How to Use This Book, page 6) and print it out.

2. Trace the pattern onto tracing paper.

3. Using the tracing-paper pattern as a guide, trace the main pieces onto the dull side of the freezer paper. Number each section as shown.

4. Cut out the freezer-paper shapes on the line.

Note: At this stage the small details on the arch and doorframe have been ignored—they will be cut out and added toward the end of the construction process.

Make tracing-paper pattern.

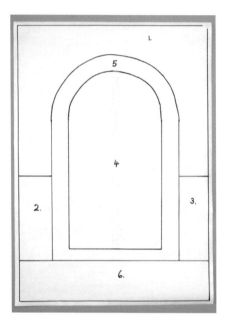

Make freezer-paper patterns.

CONSTRUCTION

Refer to Construction (page 50) as needed.

Prepare the Bases

1. With the exception of shape 1, press the freezer-paper shapes to the right side of the dark base fabric. Cut them out with a generous ½″ (1.3 cm) margin around the outside.

2. Using a fine chalk marker, draw a line around each shape, ⅛″ (3 mm) out from the edge of the freezer paper.

Make the Walls

1. Audition fabric for the main wall and press freezer-paper shape 1 to the right side of this fabric. Cut it out with a ½″ (1.3 cm) margin.

Cut out front wall.

2. Select fabric for the lower side panels. Trace shapes 2 and 3 from the back of the tracing-paper pattern onto the fusible web. Add a margin for under/overlap on all edges except the top edge.

3. Cut out the fusible web with a small margin around the drawn shape. Press it to the back of the chosen fabrics. Cut them out on the line, including the margins.

2

Add margins as indicated.

4. Peel off the backing paper and position the shapes on the corresponding dark base, leaving a ⅛″ (3 mm) margin inside the chalk line on the top edge

Prepare base and lower side panel for fusing.

Fuse lower side panel in position on base.

Make the Door

1. Select the 2 fabrics for the doors and the doorframe. Trace the door and doorframe shapes from the back of the tracing-paper pattern onto the fusible web. Add a margin for under/overlap on the outer edges of each shape.

2. Cut out and press the fusible web to the back of the door and doorframe fabric. Cut them out including the margin.

3. From the doorframe fabric that has fusible web applied to the back, cut 2 strips ⅝″ × 2½″ (1.6 cm × 6.4 cm) and 2 strips ¾″ × 2½″ (1.9 cm × 6.4 cm).

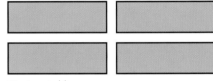

Horizontal bars

4. Position the doors on their dark base. Using the tracing-paper pattern as a guide, add the horizontal bars with the wider one below the narrower one. Stitch them in place with a straight stitch and a matching thread. Then place the doorframe in position on top and press. Stitch around the inside edges of the doorframe.

5. Choose a contrasting fabric for the center strip between the 2 doors. Apply fusible web to the back; then using a rotary cutter and ruler, cut a narrow strip ¼″ (6 mm) wide. Cut this off at the required length and press it in position.

Cut out the frame and fuse doors to base.

Make the Arch

1. Select the fabric for the arch and the foreground. Trace the arch from the back of the tracing-paper pattern onto the fusible web. Do not add any margins.

2. Cut out the fusible web arch with a small margin around the outside and press it to the back of the arch fabric. Cut out the fabric on the line.

3. Position the arch ⅛″ (3 mm) inside the chalk lines on the arch base (shape 5), and press it in place.

4. Repeat this process with the narrow strip of foreground at the base of the arch.

Position arch on base.

Make the Foreground

1. Trace the foreground shape 6. From the back of the tracing-paper pattern, trace onto the fusible web. Include the cracks in the pavement. Add a margin for under/overlap to the sides and the bottom edge.

2. Cut out this drawn shape from the fusible web with a small margin around the outside and press it onto the back of the foreground fabric.

3. Cut out the foreground as a whole then individually cut segments along the drawn lines.

4. Position the pieces in place on the foreground base, leaving a narrow gap in between each tile. Press and then straight stitch around the edge of each tile.

Position foreground in place with small gaps.

Stitch

Stitch around all the raw edges that will be visible in either a matching, contrasting, or variegated thread. Edges that will go in to a border or will be covered by the next segment do not need to be stitched

Trim

1. Press a 1″ (2.5 cm) strip of fusible web to the top edge on the back of side panel shapes 2 and 3. Trim the top edges back to ⅛″ (3 mm).

2. Apply fusible web to the back of the arch base and then trim both the inside and outside edges to ⅛″ (3 mm).

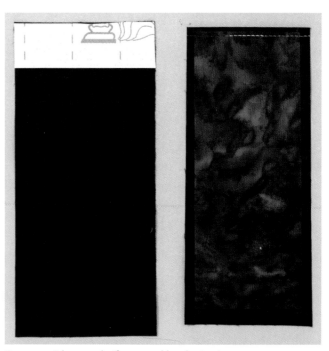

Prepare side panels (front and back view).

Put It Together

1. Trim the batting and backing fabric to 16″ × 21″ (41 cm × 53 cm) and sandwich them together (see Make the Quilt Sandwich, page 54). Place the tracing-paper pattern on the batting and mark the corners on the batting with a Sharpie. Remember to remove the basting pins as you add fabric on top.

2. With the freezer paper still attached, place the main wall (shape 1) in position, checking the placement by overlaying the pattern.

3. Place the door and door-frame segment, checking placement. Pin.

Place arch and doorframe.

4. Place the side walls in position, overlapping the bottom edge of the wall. Press them in place and then stitch along black edge using a fine, dark thread.

Add side walls and stitch.

5. Remove the freezer paper and position the trimmed arch-way over the top of the wall, side panels, and doors. Press and stitch around the edges with dark thread.

Add archway.

6. Place the foreground in place, press, and stitch.

Add foreground.

Add details.

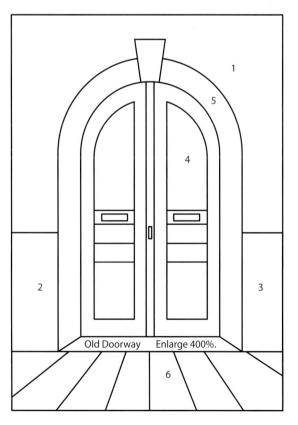

Old Doorway   Enlarge 400%.

Add the Details

1. Trace the arch decoration from the back of the pattern onto fusible web. Cut it out with a small margin around the outside and press it to the back of the arch fabric. Cut out the decoration on the line. Press it to a piece of dark fabric.

2. Stitch around the outside of the shape in a matching thread. Apply fusible web to the back and cut it out, allowing a small ⅛″ (3 mm) margin around the outside. Fuse the decoration in place on the arch.

3. Cut 2 narrow rectangles in the same fabric as the door panels and fuse them to the top horizontal bars on the doors. Likewise add a small strip to the central door strip as a handle.

Quilt and Finish

1. Quilt the main wall surface, choosing a design to replicate the chosen surface. Quilt around the edges in the doorway and in-the-ditch in the foreground. Since the quilt is small, it does not require a lot of quilting, but if you enjoy the process, you can add as much as you like.

2. Square up the quilt using a cutting board, ruler, and rotary cutter.

3. Add a narrow binding or a faced edge (see Finishing, page 95). As an alternative, have the doorway quilt framed professionally with a mat and solid frame.

ITALIAN VILLAGE   FINISHED QUILT: 17″ × 23¼″ (43 cm × 59 cm)

The brilliantly colored houses and the jewel tones of the water captivate many visitors to Italy. Venice, Burano, and the coastline of Cinque Terre have provided inspiration for painters, photographers, and of course, textile artists. The typical house is rectangular shaped and made up of the ground floor where there is a kitchen and bathroom, and a number of bedrooms upstairs.

This project is a stylized view, designed using a number of photographs taken on a very memorable trip to Italy.

Inspirational images from Burano in Italy

Fabric Requirements

Base: ¾ yard (70 cm) dark batik or similar

WALLS AND SKY

Wall 5: 8″ × 14″ (20 cm × 36 cm)

Wall 6: 5″ × 16″ (13 cm × 41 cm)

Wall 8: 7″ × 7″ (18 cm × 18 cm)

Wall 9: 7″ × 12″ (18 cm × 30 cm)

Wall 10: 5″ × 16″ (13 cm × 41 cm)

Roofs 2, 7, and 11: ¼ yard (25 cm)

Roof trim: 3″ × 12″ (8 cm × 30 cm)

Sky: 8″ × 4″ (20 cm × 10 cm)

DOORS AND WINDOWS

Glass: ¼ yard (25 cm)

White trim: ¼ yard (25 cm)

Shutters and doors: Small pieces of fabric in chosen colors

FOREGROUND

Canal 14 base fabric: 20″ × 10″ (51 cm × 25 cm)

Water: Narrow strips of fabric in assorted colors

Foot path 12: 1 strip 2″ × 20″ (5 cm × 51 cm)

Canal edge 13: 1 strip 2″ × 20″ (5 cm × 51 cm)

Boats: 3 pieces each 3″ × 6″ (8 cm × 15 cm) in 3 colors

Facing or binding: ⅓ yard (30 cm)

Backing: ⅔ yard (61 cm)

OTHER SUPPLIES

Freezer paper: 1 yard (1 m), 18″ (46 cm) wide

Tracing paper: 1 sheet 18″ × 24″ (46 cm × 61 cm) good quality 29 lb. (110 gsm)

Fusible web: 1½ yards (1.5 m), 24″-wide repositionable paper-backed (Lite Steam-A-Seam 2 or similar)

Batting: 21″ × 28″ (53 cm × 71 cm)

Threads: To blend with selected fabrics

PREPARATION

Before starting this project, read the section on Multiple Buildings (page 57).

1. Photocopy the *Italian Village* pattern (page 114). Or download the pattern (see instructions in How to Use This Book, page 6) and print it out.

2. Trace the pattern onto tracing paper.

3. Using the tracing-paper pattern as a guide, trace the main pieces onto the dull side of the freezer paper. Number each section as shown.

4. Cut out the freezer-paper shapes on the line.

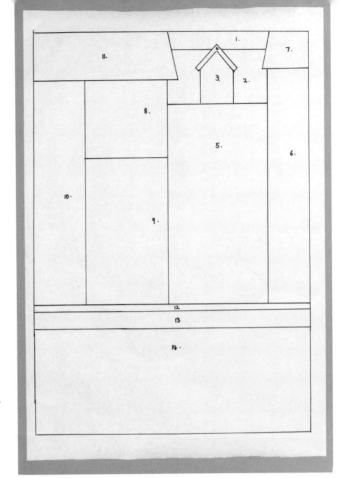

Make freezer-paper patterns.

CONSTRUCTION

Refer to Construction (page 50) as needed.

Prepare the Bases

1. Press freezer-paper shapes 2, 3, 7, 11, 12, and 13 to the right side of the dark base fabric. Cut them out with a generous ½˝ (1.3 cm) margin around the outside. *Note: Make shape 2 continuous behind the shapes 3 and 4.*

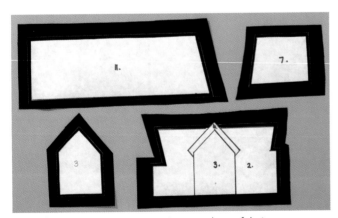

Press freezer-paper pattern pieces to base fabric.

2. Using a fine chalk marker, draw a line around each shape, ⅛˝ (3 mm) out from the edge of the freezer paper. Remove the freezer paper

Make the Walls

1. Audition fabric for the main walls 5, 6, 8, 9, and 10 and press their corresponding freezer-paper shapes to the right sides of the selected fabrics. Cut them out with a ½˝ (1.3 cm) margin for under/overlap.

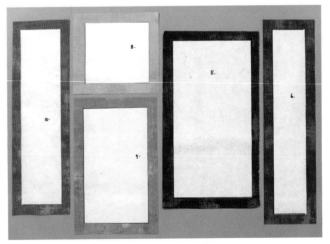

Cut out main walls.

2. Using a fine chalk marker, draw a line around each shape, ⅛˝ (3 mm) out from the edge of freezer paper. Remove the freezer paper.

Make the Doors, Windows, and Trim

1. Select fabric for the doors, doorframes, windows, and window frames.

2. Trace the door and doorframe shapes from the back of the tracing-paper pattern onto the fusible web. Add a margin for under/overlap on the outer edges of the door and on the bottom edges of the frame.

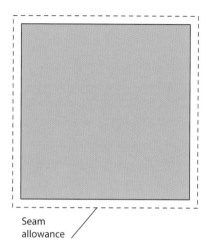

Seam allowance

Seam allowance

Trace door with margin and doorframe shapes.

3. Cut out and press the fusible web to the back of the door and door-frame fabrics. Cut them out, including the margin for under/overlap on the door and door frame.

4. Place the door and its door-frame in position on a piece of base fabric. Press it in place and trim the dark edge to ½″ (1.3 cm). Add strips of fusible web to the back of the side and back edges, and then trim ⅛″ (3 cm).

5. Repeat Steps 1–4 with the other doors and windows, stream-lining the process by pressing multiple windows and doors to 1 piece of dark fabric as needed.

Dark edges trimmed on side and top edges

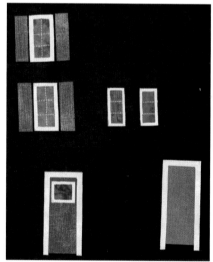

Multiple doors and windows pressed to one base

6. Cut a strip ¼″ × 6″ (0.6 cm × 15 cm) of white trim fabric backed with fusible web, and fuse to the dark fabric.

7. Prepare the extra decorative layers of the windows on wall 5 as needed.

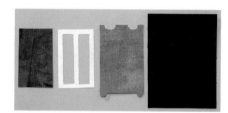

Window, window frame, decorative frame, and base

Decorative window ready to be stitched then trimmed

8. Stitch around all the raw edges that will be visible in a matching thread. As some of the framing is very narrow, a fine thread and a machine needle size 60/8 or 70/10 is a good choice. Refer to Basic Construction Notes (page 50).

9. Press all the doors, windows, and the narrow white-trim segment to fusible web and trim the edges back to ⅛″ (3 mm).

10. Peel off the backing paper and place the windows and doors in position on their corresponding walls. Press and stitch around the narrow dark borders in a fine, dark thread.

Place doors and windows on walls.

Make the Balconies

1. Trace the 2 pillars on wall 8 from the back of the pattern onto fusible web. Add an under/overlap on the outside edges.

2. Cut out the shapes with a small margin and press the fusible web to the back of the selected fabric. In the sample, it is the same fabric as wall 9. Cut out and position them on dark base fabric. Stitch around the shapes in a matching thread. The outside edges do not need stitching as they will be hidden.

Place pillars on base fabric and stitch.

3. Press fusible web to the back of the shapes and then trim back, leaving ⅛″ (3 mm) narrow edge.

4. Apply fusible web to the back of a piece of the dark base fabric and cut some narrow strips, about ⅛″ (3 mm) wide for the uprights and a strip ¼″ (6 mm) wide for the railing. Press the pieces in position, tucking the railing ends behind the pillars.

Make railing.

5. Construct the railing on wall 5 in the same way.

Make the Attic

1. Trace the pattern for wall 3 from the back of the tracing-paper pattern onto fusible web. Add a ¼″ (6 mm) margin for under/overlap on the top and bottom edges. Cut out the shape with a small margin around the outside and press it to the back of the fabric selected for this small wall.

2. Cut out the wall, including the margin on the bottom and top edges.

3. Press the piece to the corresponding base overlapping the chalk lines on the top and bottom edges.

4. Referring to Make the Doors and Windows (page 60), construct a small window and press it in place on the wall.

5. Trace shape 4 from the back of the tracing-paper pattern onto fusible web. Cut it out with a small margin and press it to the back of the white trim fabric.

Fuse attic shapes to dark base.

6. Cut out on the drawn line and then press shape 4 onto some dark base fabric. After applying fusible web to the back, cut out with a narrow edge of dark fabric around the trim.

Trim attic shapes.

Make the Roofs

1. Trace the roof shapes 2, 7, and 11 from the back of the tracing paper onto fusible web. Add an under/overlap margin where shown.

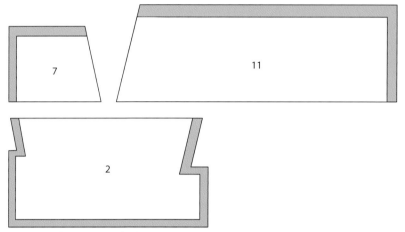

Trace roof shapes on fusible web.

2. Cut out the shapes, including the margins for under/overlap marked, with a small margin around the outside and press to the back of the selected roof fabric.

3. Cut out the shapes on the line, including the margins.

4. Press the roof shapes to their corresponding base, overlapping the chalk lines with margins where necessary.

5. Stitch along the visible edges with a straight stitch in a matching colored thread.

6. Trace the narrow strips on the roof sections from the back of the tracing-paper pattern onto fusible web. Cut them out with a small margin and press these fusible web strips to the back of the selected fabric. Cut them out on the line.

7. Press the strips to the top edge of roof 2 and the bottom edges of roof 7 and 11, overlapping roof fabric. Stitch along both edges of narrow strip to hold it in place.

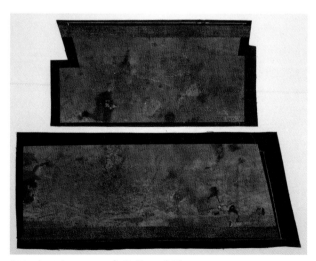

Attach strips to roofs 2, 7, and 11.

Make the Foreground

Footpath and Wall

1. Trace the foreground shapes 12 and 13 from the back of the tracing-paper pattern onto fusible web. Add a margin for under/overlap on the side and bottom edges.

Trace shapes with under/overlap margin.

2. Cut out the drawn fusible web shapes with a small margin around the outside and press them onto the back of the selected fabrics.

3. Cut them out on the line, including the under/overlap margins.

4. Position them in place on their corresponding base, ⅛″ (3 mm) inside the chalk line on the top edge and overlapping the bottom and side chalk lines.

5. Press them in place and stitch along the top edge in a matching thread.

6. Add a 1″ (2.6 cm) strip of fusible web to the top edge of the back of each strip and then trim the top edge to ⅛″ (3 mm).

Path and wall segments

Canal

1. Using freezer-paper pattern 14 as a guide, cut a piece of base fabric, allowing ½″ (1.3 cm) margin for under/overlap around the edge of the freezer paper. Choose a fabric that works well with the strips, for example a mottled blue.

2. Cut a number of strips in fabrics that have been backed with fusible web. Cut the strips in a range of widths from ¾″ (1.9 cm) to 1½″ (3.8 cm). Choose fabrics that reflect the color of the buildings and others that represent water with some horizontal patterns.

Select a range of fabrics for water.

3. Starting at the top, arrange the strips on the base fabric overlapping them to create a waterlike design. Some of the background can show through or it can be covered. Press to fuse the strips to the background.

Arrange strips for water on base.

4. Press a 1″ (2.5 cm) strip of fusible web to the top edge of the water and trim it to the top of the added strips. Fuse a 1″ (2.5 cm) strip of dark fabric to the top edge, positioning the strip under the edge with ½″ (1.3 cm) visible. Stitch in a matching thread along the water edge to hold it in place on the dark fabric.

5. Press a strip of fusible web to the back of the top edge and trim the dark edge to ⅛″ (3 mm).

Top dark edge of water trimmed

Sky

Press freezer-paper shape 1 to the selected sky fabric, making sure the color is in harmony with the water. Cut it out with a ½″ (1.3 cm) margin for under/overlap around the outside of the freezer paper.

Press freezer-paper pattern to sky fabric.

Trim the Walls

1. Refer to the diagram to determine which edges of the walls need to be trimmed and then a dark strip added.

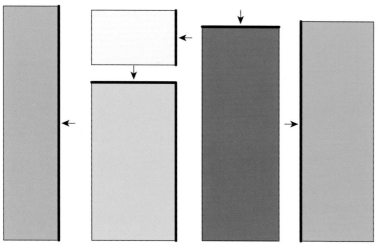

Edges marked for trimming and addition of dark strip

2. Press a 1˝ (2.5 cm) strip of fusible web to the back of the wall segment along the edge to be trimmed. Trim ⅛˝ (3 mm) inside the chalk line.

3. Cut 1˝ (2.5 cm) strips of dark base fabric and place under each of these edges. Press.

4. Stitch along the wall edge in a matching thread.

Add a dark edge.

5. Add a strip of fusible web to the back of these edges and press in place. Trim these dark colored edges to ⅛˝ (3 mm).

Put It Together

1. Trim the backing fabric to 21˝ × 28˝ (53 cm × 71 cm) and layer it with the batting and pin (see Make the Quilt Sandwich, page 54). Place the tracing-paper pattern on the batting and mark the corners on the batting with a Sharpie. Remember to remove the basting pins as you add fabric on top.

2. With the freezer paper still attached, place sky 1 in position, checking the placement by overlaying the pattern. Remove the freezer paper and pin the sky in place.

3. Place roof 2 in position, checking the placement, and press. Using a fine thread and needle, straight stitch along narrow top dark edge to hold it in place.

4. Add the subsequent walls in order, using the tracing-paper pattern to check the correct placement. Press and stitch around the edges with dark thread (see Basic Construction Notes, page 50).

Sky, roof 2, and attic in position on sandwich

Roof trim 4 and walls 5 and 6 added

Wall 10 added

Strips 12 and 13 added

6. Add the water segment, overlapping the bottom edge of the wall. Press and stitch along top dark edge.

Roof 7, walls 8 and 9, and white trim added

Roof 11 added

5. Once the edges of the buildings have been stitched down, add the narrow path and wall strips 12 and 13. Press and stitch the top edge of these strips.

Water segment added

Quilt

1. Quilt-in-the-ditch around the main features, including the doorways and windows. The walls may be quilted with an appropriate allover pattern or simply left unquilted.

2. Quilt horizontal lines on the water, making sure all the strips are fastened down. A variegated thread works well for this type of quilting.

Make the Boats

1. Trace the 3 fishing boats from the back of the tracing-paper pattern onto fusible web.

2. Cut out the shapes, leaving a small margin around the outside.

3. Press the fusible web to the back of the selected boat fabrics.

4. Cut out the boats, peel off the backing paper, and position them in the foreground. Place the darkest colored boat near the canal wall and the brightest one toward the front.

5. Fuse the boats in place and stitch around the edges. Add more quilting lines to represent the wooden sides.

Stitch wooden boats in place.

Finish

1. Square up the quilt, using a cutting board, ruler, and rotary cutter.

2. Add a narrow binding or a faced edge (see Finishing, page 95).

Italian Village
Enlarge 375%.

CAMPERVAN

FINISHED QUILT: 16½″ × 25¼″ (42 cm × 64 cm)

Known as the Kombi in Australia—or VDub, for VW or Volkswagon— the campervan has been the choice of families, backpackers, and surfers for many years. These humble vans have been decorated with flowers or customized in many other ways by their owners. Full of character and charm, these old Kombis bring a grin to people's faces and memories of wonderful childhood holidays. For quilters, they provide a wonderful facade to decorate and look idyllic in their forest setting.

For another colorway of this quilt, see Fabric (page 36).

Fabric requirements

Base: ⅓ yard (30 cm) dark batik or similar

Walls: 1 fat quarter (46 cm × 56 cm)

Roof and trim: ¼ yard (23 cm)

Wheels: ⅛ yard (11 cm)

Dark windows: 3″ × 15″ (8 cm × 38 cm)

White base: ⅔ yard (61 cm) for forest background

Tree fabric: ½ yard (0.5 m)

Background forest fabrics: 6 pieces ⅛ yard (11 cm) each, blending in a range from light to dark

Foreground: ¼ yard (23 cm)

Facing or binding: ⅓ yard (30 cm)

Backing: ⅔ yard (61 cm)

OTHER SUPPLIES

Tracing paper: 1 sheet 9″ × 18″ (23 cm × 46 cm) good quality 29 lb. (110 gsm)

Freezer paper: ½ yard (0.5 m), 18″ (46 cm) wide

Fusible web: 2 yards (2 m), 24″-wide repositionable paper-backed (Lite Steam-A-Seam 2 or similar)

Batting: 21″ × 30″ (53 cm × 76 cm)

Threads: To blend with selected fabrics

Campervan parked at beach in San Francisco

PREPARATION

1. Photocopy the *Campervan* pattern (page 122) and the *Campervan* forest pattern (page 123). Or download the patterns (see instructions in How to Use This Book, page 6) and print them out.

2. Trace the *Campervan* pattern onto tracing paper.

3. Using the tracing-paper pattern as a guide, trace the main pieces of the campervan (sections 1–6) onto the dull side of the freezer paper. Number each section as shown. The wheels and the bumper bars will be added later in the process.

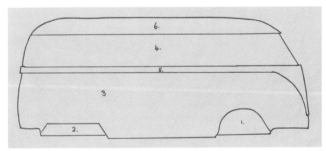

Make freezer-paper patterns.

4. Cut out the freezer-paper shapes on the line.

Make the Campervan

1. Audition fabric for the main panel and window panels. Trace shapes 3 and 4 (including windows and doors) from the back of the tracing-paper pattern onto the fusible web. Add a ¼˝ (6 mm) margin to the upper edge of the panel shape and the upper and lower edges of the window shape.

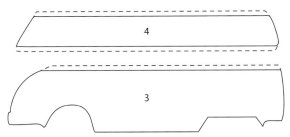

Add margins where shown.

CONSTRUCTION

Refer to Construction as needed (page 50).

Prepare the Bases

1. Press these freezer-paper shapes to the right side of the dark base fabric. Cut them out with a generous ½˝ (1.3 cm) margin for under/overlap around the outside.

2. Using a fine chalk marker, draw a line around each shape, ⅛˝ (3 mm) out from the edge of the freezer paper.

Cut out bases with ½˝ (1.3 cm) margins.

2. Cut out the fusible web with a small margin around the drawn shape and press it to the back of the selected fabric. Cut out the fusible web on the line, including the margins.

3. Cut out the door shapes on side panel 3, trimming to make ⅛˝ (3 mm) gap around the doors and the body of the campervan. Peel off the backing paper and position these pieces on the base leaving the ⅛˝ (3 mm) gap around the doors, side, and lower edges. The upper edge of this side panel will overlap the chalk line. Press.

4. Peel off the backing paper from the window section and position it on the corresponding dark base, leaving a ⅛″ (3 mm) margin inside the chalk line on the front and back and overlapping the chalk line on the top and upper and lower edge. Press.

5. Select fabric for the central trim and roof. Trace shapes 5 and 6 from the back of the tracing-paper pattern onto the fusible web. Cut out the fusible web with a small margin around the drawn shapes, then press them to the back of the chosen fabrics. Cut out the fusible web on the line.

6. Peel off the backing paper and position the trim and roof onto the corresponding dark base, leaving a ⅛″ (3 mm) margin inside the chalk line.

Place shapes on corresponding bases.

Stitch

Stitch around all the raw edges that will be visible in either a matching, contrasting, or variegated thread. Edges that will be covered by the next piece do not need to be stitched.

Trim

1. Press fusible web to the back of the panels, roof, and trim sections. Trim the edges that will be visible back to the chalk line. This should allow ⅛″ (3 mm) dark edge around each shape. Do not trim back the seam allowances.

2. Trim the inside edge of the windows to ⅛″ (3 mm), creating a narrow dark edge.

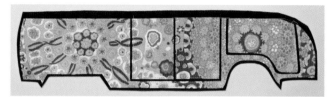

Trim to make gap around doors.

Trim inside edges of windows

3. Cut a rectangle of window fabric 11½″ × 2″ (29 cm × 5 cm) and place it behind the windows. Trim the front edge in line with front edge of window panel. Fuse it in place.

Fuse rectangle of dark fabric behind windows (back view).

Front view

4. Apply fusible web to the back of shapes 1 and 2. Trim the lower edge of these shapes just inside the chalk line.

Make the Wheels and Bumpers

1. Trace the wheels and the wheel trim from the back of the pattern onto fusible web. Cut out the shapes with a small margin around the outside of the drawn line. Choose the wheel and wheel trim fabrics and press the fusible web shapes to the back of those fabrics. Cut them out on the line and fuse the shapes to a piece of dark base fabric.

2. Repeat Step 1 for the bumper shapes 7 and 8.

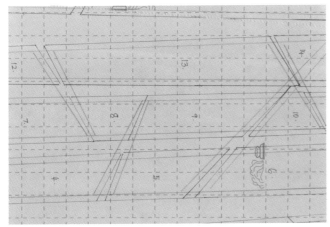

Fuse wheel and bumper shapes to base fabric.

3. Stitch around the edges of the wheels, trims, and bumpers.

4. Apply fusible web to the back of the dark fabric and cut out each shape with a narrow margin of the dark fabric as an outline.

2. From the back of the pattern, trace the forest shapes onto fusible web. Add ¼″ (6 mm) seam allowance around each shape. Include the numbers on each shape. Cut them out, leaving a margin around each fusible web shape.

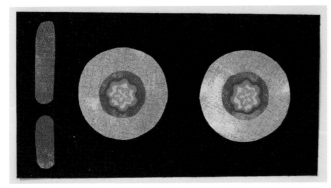

Trace forest shapes on fusible web.

Make the Forest Background

1. Trace the forest pattern onto the right side of a piece of white fabric, using a lightbox, window, or whatever you have available.

Trace pattern on white fabric base.

3. Audition fabrics for the forest that work well with the planned color scheme for the campervan. Select fabrics that have a range of value and some contrast in pattern but also harmonize well together.

Audition fabrics.

4. Select fabrics for each forest piece, generally using the lighter color fabrics near the horizon line gradually working toward the darker fabrics at the top. Press the appropriate fusible web shape onto the back of the selected fabrics. Cut out each piece on the line that includes the seam allowance.

5. Peel off the backing paper and place each piece in position on the white fabric base overlapping the drawn tree lines.

6. Keep adding the pieces to their corresponding places on the white base. When all the pieces are in place press to fuse these shapes to the white base.

Position pieces on white fabric.

Fuse pieces to background fabric.

7. From the back of the pattern, trace the trunks onto fusible web, leaving a small gap in between. Number each trunk according to the pattern. Add a ½″ (1.3 cm) seam allowance to the top and bottom of each trunk shape. Cut out the fusible web with a small margin around each shape. Press the trunk shapes to the back of the selected fabric. Cut out the shapes including under/overlaps.

8. Remove the backing paper and place the trunks in position on the white base. Check that the edges of the foliage shapes are covered, and then press lightly to fuse the trunks in place.

9. Repeat Steps 7 and 8 to place the branches, tucking the ends under the trunks.

Fuse trunks in place making sure edges of foliage are covered.

Make the Foreground

1. Select the fabric and cut 1 strip 6½″ × 18″ (17 cm × 46 cm).

2. Fuse a 1″ (2.5 cm) strip of fusible web to the top edge (on the back) and then trim off ¼″ (6 mm).

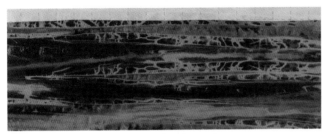

Trim top edge of foreground (back view).

Put It Together

Background

1. Trim the batting and backing fabric to 21″ × 30″ (53 cm × 76 cm) and layer them together (see Make the Quilt Sandwich, page 54).

2. Place the forest background in position on the batting.

3. Using a walking foot, straight stitch along the edge of the trees, stitching through the sandwich. Quilt the foliage sections as desired.

Quilt sections of foliage

4. Remove the backing paper from fusible web on the top edge of the foreground and place it in position. Press and then stitch along the top edge.

5. Add more horizontal quilting to the foreground, using the pattern in the fabric as a guide.

Stitch foreground.

Campervan

1. Using the *Campervan* tracing-paper pattern as a guide, place sections 1 and 2 in position. Press and stitch the lower straight edge.

2. Fuse the wheels in position and stitch around the outside on the narrow dark edge. Stitch with a matching fine dark thread and appropriate needle. Refer to Basic Construction Notes (page 50).

Position and stitch wheels in place.

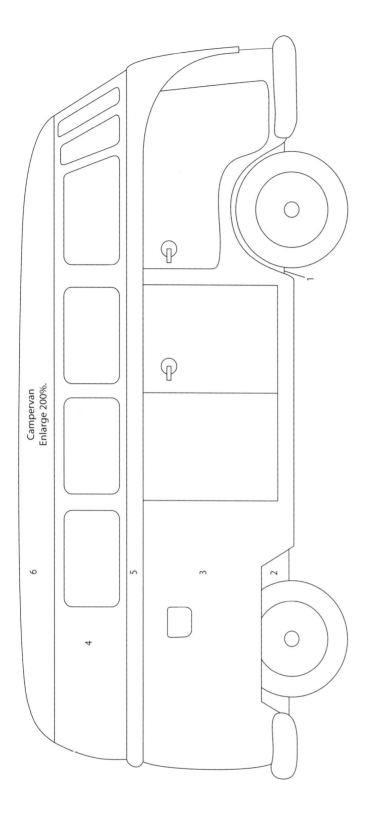

Campervan
Enlarge 200%.

6

5

4

3

2

1

3. Fuse the main body of the campervan and the window section in position. Stitch around dark edges.

Add main body.

Add windows.

4. Fuse the roof and the trim, overlapping where appropriate. Stitch around the edge.

5. Fuse the bumpers in place and stitch.

Fuse and stitch the remaining pieces.

Quilt and Finish

1. Stitch around the cut out windows and the dark outlines on the main panels. Add more quilting if desired.

2. Square up the quilt, using a cutting board, ruler, and rotary cutter.

3. Add a facing (see Finishing, page 95).

Campervan Forest
Enlarge 300%.

student GALLERY QUILTS

All Souls Church by Beth McCrystal, 20″ × 23″ (51 cm × 58 cm)

Italy by Carol Ellrott, 27½″ × 21½″ (70 cm × 55 cm)

Laufas Turf Houses, Iceland by Harriet Wilson, 28¾″ × 18½″ (73 cm × 47 cm)

Photo by Neil Porter

Incineration Plant Vienna (after Hundertwasser) by Janet Scotton, 24˝ × 33˝ (61 cm × 84 cm)

Tabard House by Sandy Hathaway, 16˝ × 24˝ (41 cm × 61 cm)

My House by Monica Hainer, 19½˝ × 14½˝ (50 cm × 37 cm)

Norfolk House by Yvonne Watson, 23˝ × 16˝ (58 cm × 41 cm)

Venice Remembered by Deborah Lamb-Mechanick, 23½″ × 40″ (60 cm × 102 cm)

Amsterdam by Margaret Ruiter, 16⅝″ × 23⅝″ (42 cm × 60 cm)

My New Sewing Room by Chrys Schock, 25½″ × 18¾″ (65 cm × 48 cm)

about the AUTHOR

Gloria Loughman lives by the sea on the beautiful Bellarine Peninsula in Victoria, Australia. Married with three daughters, she is a trained secondary teacher, having worked mainly in literacy and special education faculties. Her initiation into the world of patchwork occurred approximately 29 years ago, when she was recovering from surgery and chemotherapy for breast cancer.

Over the years she has dabbled in many areas, including strip piecing, bargello, colorwash, fabric dyeing and painting, and machine embroidery. After completing studies in design and color as part of a diploma of art in 1996, she began to make her large vivid landscape quilts depicting the Australian bush. These quilts have won many major awards in Australia, Europe, Japan, and the United States. Her quilt *Kimberley Mystique* was the winner of Australia's most prestigious national quilting award in 2003.

Gloria loves sharing her knowledge and skills with others. Known to take people outside their comfort zone, Gloria is adept at pushing boundaries while still managing to instill confidence. Many students come back for a second or third class. Gloria's commitment to teaching was acknowledged when she received the 2009 Rajah Award for her outstanding contribution to quiltmaking in Australia.

In addition to being in demand as a teacher, Gloria has curated exhibitions of Australian quilts in the United States and has had the privilege of judging at many major shows. Her work has been featured in many books and magazines.

What began as a therapy has developed into a passion and has given Gloria the opportunity to travel the world exhibiting her quilts, teaching classes, and meeting a lot of wonderful people.

Gloria's website: glorialoughman.com

ALSO BY GLORIA LOUGHMAN

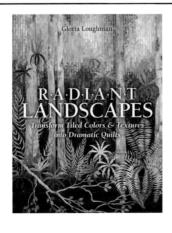

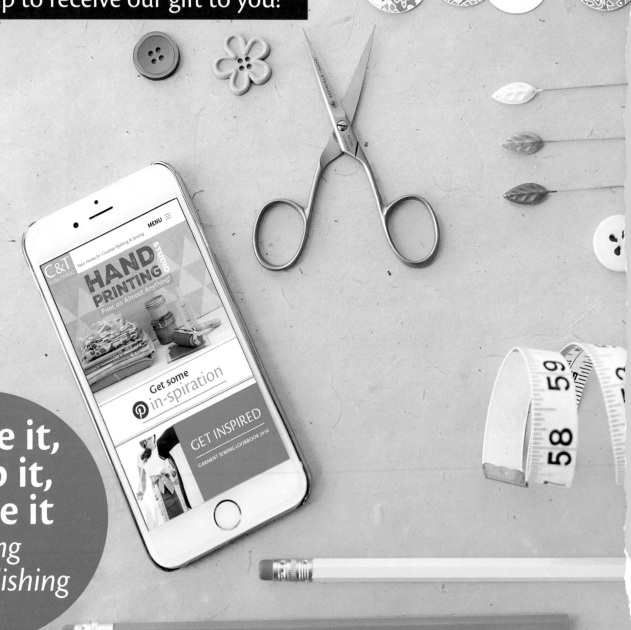

Want even more creative content?

Make it,
snap it,
share it
using
#ctpublishing